DIANA'S REBEL HERITAGE

DIANA'S REBEL HERITAGE

Five Centuries of Scandal and Defiance

HISTORY

by Gail Douglas

PUBLISHED BY ALTITUDE PUBLISHING CANADA LTD.
1500 Railway Avenue, Canmore, Alberta T1W 1P6
www.altitudepublishing.com
1-800-957-6888

Extreme care has been taken to ensure that all information presented in
this book is accurate and up to date. Neither the author nor the
publisher can be held responsible for any errors.

Publisher	Stephen Hutchings
Associate Publisher	Kara Turner
Series Editor	Jill Foran
Editor	Pat Kozak

We acknowledge the financial support of the Government
of Canada through the Book Publishing Industry Development
Program (BPIDP) for our publishing activities.

Altitude GreenTree Program
Altitude Publishing will plant twice as many trees as were used
in the manufacturing of this product.

National Library of Canada Cataloguing in Publication Data

Douglas, Gail
  Diana's rebel heritage / Gail Douglas.

(Amazing stories)
ISBN 1-55265-901-1

  1. Diana, Princess of Wales, 1961-1997. 2. Spencer family.
3. Princesses--Great Britain--Biography. I. Title. II. Series:
Amazing stories (Canmore, Alta.)

DA591.A45D53345 2005   941.085'092   C2005-901006-1

An application for the trademark for Amazing Stories™
has been made and the registered trademark is pending.

Printed and bound in Canada by Friesens

2 4 6 8 9 7 5 3 1

For Molly

Contents

Prologue

Sarah Churchill was in mortal peril. Guards stood outside the royal quarters at the residence where she served as lady-in-waiting to Princess Anne, King James II's daughter.

The outspoken Sarah had been too free with her criticisms of the king, and her soldier husband had deserted the monarch. Furious, King James had ordered her arrest. As soon as his soldiers arrived with the warrant, she would be charged with treason and taken to the Tower of London to await trial. The penalty for treason was execution.

Princess Anne and two other women were in an upstairs room with Sarah; they were allies, not jailers. Anticipating the king's actions, Sarah had devised an escape plan. Using a secret staircase expressly built for the purpose, the nervous foursome crept down to a door that opened onto a side street.

As arranged, two men were waiting in the shadows. These accomplices guided the women through the dark, dirty streets of London to a meeting point where they boarded a hackney coach. Cold, mud-splashed and terrified, they collapsed inside the coach, hardly daring to speak until they arrived at the home of the former Archbishop of Canterbury. From there, they began the last leg of their journey accompanied by 40 horsemen.

Even with this armed escort, the fugitives breathed freely only when they reached Nottingham and found a crowd of cheering citizens lining the streets to greet them. That evening, Sarah and her co-conspirators attended a banquet to celebrate their safe arrival and the start of the "Glorious Revolution" of 1688.

It was a pivotal moment for the country and the monarchy, not to mention for Sarah Churchill. On the night of the escape, and during the years to come, Sarah demonstrated a truth that might well have inspired her descendant Diana, Princess of Wales, nearly 300 years later.

Sarah proved that even a powerful monarchy is no match for a woman of courage and spirit.

Introduction

t all seemed so romantic. "Here is the stuff of which fairytales are made", the Archbishop of Canterbury gushed as he presided over the wedding of Lady Diana Spencer and Charles, Prince of Wales at London's St Paul's Cathedral on 29 July 1981.

To the millions of royal-watchers in the cathedral, lining the streets of London and glued to their television sets around the world, the ceremony with all its glittering pageantry indeed represented the happy ending of a Cinderella fantasy.

It took a few years for them to realise that it was actually the unhappy beginning of a classic tragedy. The real-life Prince Charming was in love with someone other than his obscure kindergarten-teacher bride.

However, she'd always been more than just an obscure kindergarten teacher. Diana Spencer was a member of the innermost circle of the British aristocracy, her family so deeply rooted in England's soil her pedigree made her new in-laws look like recent immigrants.

The Spencers and their gigantic network of relatives have figured prominently in their country's fortunes for at least five centuries and possibly for the better part of the past millennium, and their tumultuous relationship with British royalty goes back just as far.

Diana's ancestors include monarchs and mistresses, courtiers and courtesans, the venerated and the venal. The matchmakers who expected the new princess to submit meekly to an entrenched tradition of princely privilege and wifely duty obviously hadn't taken into account the mutinous blood coursing through her veins.

Diana was just a girl, barely out of her teens, when she took that fateful trip to the altar, but the potential for the charismatic international icon she became was embedded in her genes and – if anyone had troubled to look for it – in a multitude of history books.

Chapter 1
The Founding Mothers

o scamper through the branches and off-shoots of Diana Spencer's family tree is to find dozens of fascinating stories squir-reled away in all its nooks and crannies. The Spencer roots have been preserved through an unbroken line of male heirs, but the sections grafted on through marriage from other ancestral trees offer the best dramatic pickings.

The background of Diana's 11 times great-grandmother, for example, holds a sad tale. Margaret Willoughby, wealthy heiress of an important Tudor-era family, married Diana's ancestor, the sheep-farming magnate Baron Robert Spencer. Margaret's first cousin once removed was Lady Jane Grey, England's tragic "nine days queen".

A petite, fair-haired, freckle-faced young woman who preferred reading Plato in the original Greek to dabbling in court intrigues, Lady Jane was pushed into the royal spotlight because she was a cousin of Henry VIII's uncontested heir, Edward VI.

Edward was a frail boy when he became England's monarch and the question of his eventual successor was hotly disputed. His half-sister Mary Tudor, Henry's daughter from his first marriage, seemed the logical choice. But the Duke of Northumberland, Lord Protector of the realm during the latter part of the young king's minority, didn't look forward to losing his position as the power behind the throne if Mary became queen. He decided to plan for a succession better suited to his purposes.

Northumberland's first move was to arrange a marriage between his son and Lady Jane Grey. Within three days of Edward's death, Northumberland had declared Jane the new monarch.

But Northumberland had underestimated Mary Tudor, who mustered an army and nine days later had seized the throne. Although Lady Jane had protested all along that the crown was rightfully Mary's, the hapless girl was sent to the Tower of London and ultimately lost her head, as did her young husband, his father and several others accused of plotting against Mary.

The subsequent persecution of Protestants during Queen Mary's reign earned her the nickname "Bloody Mary".

The Founding Mothers

By the time she died and her Protestant half-sister, Elizabeth, ascended the throne, an abhorrence of Roman Catholicism was so deeply ingrained in the English psyche it would torment the country for centuries to come.

Lady Jane Grey's portrait hangs at the Spencer estate of Althorp in Northamptonshire, reputedly the only image painted of her during her short lifetime. But Lady Jane wasn't the only young woman in Diana's ancestry who lost her head for the sake of a crown. Two of Diana's distant kinswomen, Anne Boleyn and Catherine Howard, were wives of Henry VIII and went to the block when His Royal Majesty was displeased with them. Diana was also a direct descendant of Mary (Stuart), Queen of Scots, whose head was chopped off by order of her cousin, Queen Elizabeth I.

Given all those ghosts wandering through her heritage with their heads tucked underneath their arms, it's a mystery why Diana wasn't more leery of tangling with royalty.

Not all the women who found their way into the Spencer pedigree were victims, however. Several were indomitable heroines, others were tough cookies in spite of the male-dominated worlds they inhabited, and some, like Diana, were a mercurial mixture of strength and vulnerability.

In the "tough cookie" category, the first entry has to be the Tudor tycoon in the Cavendish branch of the Spencer tree.

The Other "Queen Bess"

Elizabeth of Hardwick, nicknamed Bess, was one of five

children born to a family that had farmed in Derbyshire since the 13th century. Her father died before Elizabeth was a year old. Although her mother remarried, finances remained tight.

Bess was 12 when she went into service in the London household of a prominent Derbyshire family in the early 1500s. There she met Robert Barlow, a young man not much older than herself, who was in service in the same household. Robert became ill and Bess nursed him. He fell in love with her and they married when she was just 13. Bess was too young, and Robert was too sick, for the union to be consummated. When Robert died a year later, Bess received a widow's pension amounting to one-third of his income.

The young widow was serving in the household of Lady Jane Grey's mother when she met her second husband, William Cavendish. He had acquired grants of church land in return for his work as a commissioner responsible for the dissolution of monasteries during the Protestant Reformation and was exceedingly well-off. Although William was 22 years older than Bess he was her one true love, and they produced six surviving children from their marriage.

Bess persuaded William to sell the monastery lands and move to her home county of Derbyshire. There they built a large house that was the predecessor of Chatsworth House, the ancestral home of the Dukes of Devonshire and the 18th-century domain of one of Diana's most charismatic forebears, Georgiana Spencer Cavendish, Duchess of Devonshire. William taught Bess all she needed to know about accounting and estate management, leaving her well-qualified to run her own business affairs.

After William Cavendish passed away, Bess was appointed lady-in-waiting to Queen Elizabeth. At court she met and married another generous William, a wealthy and trusted friend of the queen named Sir William St Loe. Widowed twice, Sir William had children of his own and a brother who'd expected to be his heir, even though the two men didn't get along. Perhaps that was why the brother tried to poison Bess and William – fortunately without success. When Sir William died five years into the marriage, he left all his lands to Bess and her children.

In 1567, Bess married her last husband, George Talbot, the sixth Earl of Shrewsbury, who was regarded at the time as the richest nobleman in England and owned numerous estates. (In 1658, further links between their families were forged when two of his children married two of hers in a double ceremony.)

In 1569, Queen Elizabeth placed the Earl of Shrewsbury in charge of guarding Mary, Queen of Scots, a duty he retained until Mary's death 15 years later. During those years Mary was imprisoned in one or another of the Shrewsbury estates and the responsibility created considerable tension in Bess's marriage.

Every time a threat came to light of someone planning either to harm Mary or rescue her, the whole household packed up and moved to a different estate. Furthermore,

Mary Stuart was beautiful and charming, and Bess wasn't immune to jealousy.

Bess, a resourceful woman, coped with her pangs of possessiveness by making a special effort to befriend Mary, and the two of them whiled away many hours chatting over their embroidery and tapestry work. Their friendship seems to have been rather superficial, though. Mary tended to play the couple off against each other and aggravate their problems, while Bess was prepared to use Mary to lash out at the earl.

From about 1580, Bess and her husband were separated on and off, but the crisis came in 1583 when Bess learned that her husband was having an affair – not with Mary but with a serving wench named Eleanor Britton. Bess reportedly started a rumour, spread by two of her Cavendish sons, that the Earl of Shrewsbury had betrayed his monarch's trust by having an affair with Queen Mary, a liaison that had produced two children.

Queen Elizabeth promptly sent for Bess and her sons and questioned them. Before her interrogation was over, they were on their knees swearing that the stories were nothing but malicious rumours created and spread by other people. Elizabeth then required them to sign a written declaration that Mary Stuart had not given birth to any child since her arrival in England.

Bess wrote to her husband expressing regret for her behaviour, but he refused to forgive her. That same year, Bess bought her old home at Hardwick from her debt-ridden brother and put it in her son William's name. At that point, her long-term plan was that he would inherit the house after her death.

Queen Mary was assigned to a new jailer in 1584, and three years later met her untimely death. Her execution brought Bess and her husband back together for a brief period, but there was to be no permanent reconciliation. The earl left once and for all and went to live with Eleanor Britton.

Bess had begun restoring Old Hardwick Hall in 1585, but abandoned the project after 1590 when the earl died and left her all his assets. Suddenly she was the richest woman in England, other than Queen Elizabeth. Owner of acres of pasturage, mineral and timber rights, iron and glass works, coal pits and smithies, Bess was also mistress of a castle, a manor house and estates in Staffordshire, Derbyshire and Yorkshire.

The new Hardwick Hall featured six projecting towers at the sides of the rectangular house, each tower decorated with a large crest bearing the initials "ES" for Elizabeth of Shrewsbury, in case anyone didn't know whose great achievement it was. Windows dominated the façade, inspiring a popular rhyme, "Hardwick Hall, more glass than wall".

Bess moved into the house in 1597 and remained there until her death in 1608 at the age of 90. Although the Old Hall remains only as ruins today, Bess's mansion still stands, queening it over the surrounding countryside.

Throughout her life, Bess of Hardwick was embroiled in dramas at Queen Elizabeth's court. Bess herself ended up in the Tower on two separate occasions for annoying the touchy monarch. The first time was when she encouraged the marriage of her daughter to a Stuart heir without the Queen's permission. The second occasion was when she refused to report to the sovereign what she knew about the secret marriage and pregnancy of Lady Catherine Grey, the late Lady Jane's sister, to Edward Seymour.

Queen Elizabeth didn't take kindly to clandestine romances between her courtiers and maids of honour, and Bess wasn't the only person who found that out the hard way.

A mysterious "Dark Lady" hidden in another branch of the Spencer tree learned the same lesson.

Shady Lady

Elizabeth Vernon was a lady-in-waiting in the court of Queen Elizabeth I, where dashing privateers and handsome lords paid homage to the Virgin Queen.

Henry Wriothesley, the third Earl of Southampton, had grown up at court. His long golden hair and finely chiselled features belied the disposition of a firebrand, and although he was known for wading into brawls at the slightest provocation, he was still one of the queen's favourites.

He was exactly the kind of man who would make a young lady's pulse race, so when he noticed Mistress Vernon she apparently forgot to be careful, forgot that she was treading on the queen's turf, forgot everything but the giddy joy of being in love.

The inevitable happened and when Southampton, off in Paris, learned that he was about to become a father, he rushed home to make an honest woman of his lover. They married in secret, which must have been a huge relief to the mother-to-be.

But Queen Elizabeth heard about their elopement and reacted exactly as they should have expected. She sent the earl to the Tower of London and had his pregnant bride tossed into Fleet prison.

They weren't locked up for long, but their careers at court were finished and the episode hardened Southampton against the despotic old virago who held so much power over her subjects. He'd already been drawn to another of the queen's disenchanted favourites, the Earl of Essex, and was ready to join the band of grumbling lords chafing under the sovereign's iron rule.

Southampton's great passion, besides finding and making trouble, was literature. He was a patron of several writers, including William Shakespeare, who had dedicated two works of poetry to him – *Venus and Adonis* and *The Rape of Lucrece*. Experts have argued that Shakespeare's sonnets were addressed to Southampton as well, but the evidence is inconclusive on that issue. Another popular theory is that the "Dark Lady" of the sonnets is the earl, with a little gender-bending to obscure his identity. But one scholar suggests that Elizabeth Vernon, Countess Southampton, was the real "Dark Lady" and, furthermore, was Shakespeare's lover and gave birth to *his* child, not Southampton's.

That child was a little girl named Penelope who grew up and married William Spencer, son of Baron Robert Spencer of Althorp. Elizabeth Vernon, therefore, was Diana Spencer's 10 times great-grandmother. And if the controversial theory of Elizabeth as the "Dark Lady" is correct, William Shakespeare is the 10 times great-grandfather of Diana and therefore 11 times great-grandfather of her son William, who is currently second in line to the British throne.

However, the prince's given name is neither a nod to his Spencer ancestors nor to William Shakespeare. The name William found its way to the English throne after the Battle of Hastings in 1066, when William the Conqueror led his Norman troops to a decisive victory and made himself king.

According to Spencer tradition, their family can be traced back to a key member of the Conqueror's entourage – Robert Despenser.

The Spencer Roots

The Norman word for "steward" is "despenser". So Robert, who was steward to the household of William the Conqueror, went by the name of Robert Despenser. Robert's descendants were fierce warriors but eventually the Norman prefix was dropped in favour of the abbreviated Spencer, and the dissonance of clashing swords gave way to the tranquil bleating of lambs.

The Spencers became sheep farmers in pre-Tudor

times, putting their flocks out to graze on leased land in Warwickshire. They earned a comfortable living and carved out a niche in respectable society, systematically enhancing their position by marrying into the professional and land-owner classes.

At the start of the 16th century, English wool was a hot commodity throughout Europe so John Spencer, the man the family calls "the Founder", seized the opportunity to turn his operation into big business. When the Warwickshire estate of Wormleighton came up for sale, he bought it for cash. He enlarged its manor house and made it the Spencer family seat and the centre of his sheep-farming empire.

In 1508 a tract of land John was leasing in Northamptonshire went up for sale, so he purchased it for £800. He called it Althorp, probably based on a local Saxon name, and decided to build a manor house there. He improved the grounds of both estates and created a park where, before the end of the century, his grandson would plant oak trees to supply shipbuilders in the event of new threats from the Spanish Armada.

The trees, never called into service for shipbuilding, still stood as silent sentinels when Diana, Princess of Wales returned to Althorp in 1997 for the last time.

John harboured aristocratic ambitions for himself and future Spencers and he worked hard to achieve them. First, he earned a knighthood for himself and his heirs. Then, he had his genealogy traced and won the right for his family to bear the ancient Despenser arms. Finally, he arranged for the construction of a tomb befitting a nobleman and his descendants in the Church of St Mary in Great Brington, near Althorp House.

The Spencers who followed John did him proud. By the late 1500s, the richest man in the country was said to be John's descendant, Sir Robert Spencer. However, because Queen Elizabeth I was reluctant to create new titles, a peerage was out of reach.

The situation changed when the queen died in 1603 and James VI of Scotland ascended the English throne as James I. The new king was perfectly willing to expand the aristocracy. By selling titles he could raise money for his lavish lifestyle without having to apply to parliament for funds.

Before long, Sir Robert was Baron Spencer and had accepted a diplomatic posting on the Continent. He found he didn't care for court life in Europe and was even less impressed by the sycophancy and questionable morality he saw in the English palace. When King James offered him an earldom, he politely turned it down and beat a path back home to the lush green fields of Northamptonshire.

Taking his seat in the House of Lords, he became an outspoken critic of the monarch's "Divine Right of Kings" philosophy, which held that God had appointed kings to rule their subjects, and monarchs were therefore infallible. King James firmly believed that parliament had no business criticising or questioning him.

Robert found an ally in another member of the House, Henry Wriothesley, third Earl of Southampton (the dashing courtier who married Elizabeth Vernon), who had come within a hair of losing his head towards the end of Elizabeth's reign. He'd supported the rebellion of the Earl of Essex by persuading the players of the Globe Theatre to revive *Richard II*, a play about the justifiable overthrow of a king, on the very eve of the uprising.

The queen, not amused, had stripped Southampton of his titles and again sent him to the Tower. Only the intervention of a friend at court had saved his neck, but he faced life in prison.

King James, however, set Southampton free, reinstating his peerage and showering him with new honours. Even so, Southampton was critical of his monarch's Divine Right doctrine. Because his views were so similar to Spencer's, the two men became friends and cemented their alliance by officially joining their families. Robert Spencer's son William needed a wife. Penelope Wriothesley, Southampton's daughter, seemed perfect.

And she was.

First Lady of Althorp

Pretty, pragmatic Penelope, who was known for her intelligence and energy, must have relished the sweet simplicity of life in the country with William Spencer.

Penelope and William were married in 1614 and went

to live at Althorp with the widowed Robert, whose wife, Margaret, had died in childbirth in 1597. The bride took one look at the way her father-in-law's steward and bailiff were handling the accounts of the household, stables, park and farms and announced that they wouldn't do. They weren't precise enough.

Baron Robert didn't tell Penelope to stay out of his business. Instead, he handed her the day-to-day administration of the estate and gave her a free hand to organise things her way.

Penelope introduced new methods of tracking expenditures and controlling inventory and began attracting exceptional employees by offering salaries double and sometimes triple the going rate. Her household servants wore the finest livery and, like all their employees, were treated with respect. All she asked in return was excellence – and she usually got it.

Penelope and William widened their network of acquaintances by entertaining lavishly and with great panache, their guests drawn from the ranks of royalty, aristocratic circles, the hunting and horse-racing crowd, professional people and local friends.

She kept up with new trends in hospitality and must have been the talk of the countryside when she placed dinner forks on her table along with the conventional knives and spoons. The new utensil, which had been around for hundreds of years in parts of the world such as Persia, and had made its way only gradually to Italy and then France, didn't catch on at first in England. Englishmen sniffed that using the fool thing was an unmanly Italian affectation. There could be no greater condemnation.

As the Althorp guest list grew, Penelope and William decided they needed still more space, so they worked together to plan another enlargement of Althorp. Then Penelope started sprucing up the grounds with vegetable and flower gardens, while William put in a racecourse in the estate's park.

Somehow, Penelope found the time and stamina to bear 13 children, seven of whom survived to adulthood. The oldest son was Henry, presumably named for Penelope's father, who had died of the plague while tilting at Catholic windmills in The Netherlands.

Baron Robert died in 1627 and was laid to rest in the Spencer Chapel in the church at Great Brington. Nine years later William Spencer died at just 44 years old, leaving Penelope devastated. Henry rushed home from Oxford where, by the age of 16, he'd already earned a Master of Arts degree.

Until he was 18, Henry remained under the guardianship of his mother and her brother Thomas Wriothesley, but once he was on his own he set out to find a bride.

The Sweet One

It didn't take Henry long to find the love of his life – Dorothy Sidney, daughter of Robert Sidney, Earl of Leicester. Dorothy, like her eight times great-granddaughter Diana, was a sparkling blonde with riveting blue eyes, a peaches-and-cream complexion and, by all accounts, a glow from within that lit up any room she entered.

Henry and Dorothy were deeply in love and remained devoted to each other throughout their marriage. Their story must have been familiar to Diana, and with such a tale in her own family background it's no wonder she believed that marriage and eternal love really could exist outside a Barbara Cartland romance novel.

At Diana's funeral in 1997, almost 400 years after Henry and Dorothy began their married life, the popular recording artist Elton John performed a reworked version of a song he had written years earlier, *Goodbye England's Rose*. The words are a ghostly echo of *Go Lovely Rose*, a verse originally written for Dorothy by an admirer, the poet Edmund Waller.

Edmund was hopelessly in love with Dorothy and, before she married Henry, had courted her with his flirtatious, sometimes suggestive, rhymes. He called her *Sacharissa* – the sweet one.

But even if she was flattered by his attention, she didn't return his romantic feelings. Nor would she have been bowled over by his poetic talents. Dorothy's world was packed with literary lights, including her grandfather, an aunt, a great-aunt and, the most celebrated of all, her great-uncle Sir Philip Sidney, the famous Elizabethan poet.

When Henry proposed to Dorothy, he was only 19, a

little younger than his bride-to-be. But he was mature and sensible and had a spotless reputation, unusual among his peers. An articulate conversationalist, Henry had been seasoned by debates among his fellow intellectuals at Oxford and had no trouble holding his own among the sophisticated Sidneys. He was also good-looking, rich and – by this time – fully in charge of his inheritance.

The young lovers exchanged vows on 20 July 1639 at the Sidney family's ancestral home of Penshurst in Kent, a setting so romantic it remains a favourite location for weddings to this day.

The couple went to live with Dorothy's parents in Paris, where her father was ambassador to the court of Louis XIII. When they returned two years later with their two small children, Dorothy and Robert, they were still very much in love and looking forward to a rosy future.

But they found their country in the process of tearing itself apart. It would do the same to them.

The Reluctant Cavalier
By early January 1642, King Charles I and his subjects were preparing to make war on each other. Although Charles was a decent man and a dedicated monarch, he'd committed some serious blunders. He and his ministers were widely despised and he was more contemptuous of parliament than his father had ever been.

Much of the conflict was rooted in religion. Charles

had offended the Scots by trying to impose the Anglican prayer book on their Presbyterian churches, and a law that allowed only Anglicans to hold government office offended everybody except that select group. Furthermore, a rumour that Charles had secretly converted to Catholicism made him unpopular throughout the Catholic-fearing country.

Ranged against the king and his supporters were the Independents, who wanted to do away with the Anglican Church, and the Presbyterians who thought the Anglican Church could be reformed along the lines of the Scottish Church. Both groups came under the general umbrella term, "Puritans". More extreme were "the Levellers", who called for annual sessions of parliament, payment for members and the franchise for all householders. These demands, which may seem reasonable now, were considered radical and even dangerous at that time.

Henry Spencer held liberal political ideas and believed in religious toleration, even though he was Anglican and his father had been rigidly anti-Puritan. But to take up arms against the anointed king was something Henry couldn't condone.

Most of the country remained neutral, the average person being too busy trying to make ends meet to get involved in political wrangling. In general, though, the royalist strength was in the north and west, while the Independents who dominated the parliamentary army held sway over the south and around London.

When matters came to a head, Henry set aside his reservations and allied himself with the Royalists, known as Cavaliers. His father-in-law, Lord Leicester, came to the same decision. But two of Lord Leicester's sons, Philip and Algernon Sidney, went with the Parliamentarians, dubbed Roundheads for the short, bowl-like haircuts of the Puritans.

King Charles raised his standard at Nottingham in August 1642 as a call for loyal followers to rally to his cause. Meanwhile, the parliamentary commander was also preparing for war.

Henry Spencer couldn't muster a regiment for His Majesty since almost his entire shire was allied with the Parliamentarians. He moved his family to the Leicester stronghold of Penshurst and then rode to Nottingham to volunteer for an existing regiment. It was a wise move. Roundheads occupied Althorp within days.

Henry made no bones about wishing he could turn his back on the whole sorry business. "If there could be an expedient found to salve the punctilio of honour, I would not continue here an hour," he told his wife when he wrote to her. Nevertheless, he attached himself to the cavalry unit led by the king's nephew, Prince Rupert of the Rhine, and prepared to face some of his closest friends and philosophical soulmates in battle.

On 22 October the Royalists reached Edgehill, a low ridge close to the Spencer family seat of Wormleighton. Henry entertained Prince Rupert at the estate on the eve of battle and arranged to advance the cash-strapped king £10,000 to support the war effort. The next day he was at the forefront of the cavalry charge of Prince Rupert's Cavaliers as they thundered headlong into the enemy flank, scattering them in all directions.

The battle ended with both the Royalists and the Parliamentarians claiming victory. Yet both had sustained huge losses. The battlefield was strewn with dead and wounded soldiers who were plundered during the night – their pockets searched for valuables, their clothes stripped from their bodies.

In a lull after the battle, Henry managed to get a leave of absence to head for Penshurst to visit his family. Dorothy's joyful relief on seeing her husband riding up to the castle is easy to imagine, but the respite lasted only a few short months. Henry had to rejoin the royalist troops at Oxford in the spring of 1643. The king had set up headquarters in the quiet university town, filling it with the sights and sounds of troops drilling in college quadrangles and Cavaliers clattering through the streets on their great chargers.

In June, Henry received a new title in recognition of his loyalty – and probably as thanks for his loan. Convinced he wasn't likely to see his £10,000 again, Henry graciously accepted the earldom his grandfather had refused, reviving a defunct title to become the first Earl of Sunderland.

As the war progressed, Henry became more disillusioned, more depressed, more certain that the conflict was an exercise in futility. He told Dorothy in a letter that no matter who won, it would be "a victory for violent and extreme men".

On 16 September 1643, the Royalists regrouped at Oxford. Henry wrote to Dorothy telling her he'd decided he would never accept a commission in the Royalist army but would focus on personally protecting the king. He ended the letter with the affectionate sign-off, "Most passionately and perfectly yours, Sunderland."

Four days later he was hit in the groin with a cannon shot. Death took its time claiming the young Cavalier. He died in agony for a cause he no longer condoned. He was 23 years old.

The Heroine of Althorp
Dorothy was pregnant with her third child and close to her delivery date when one of her father's servants brought word to Penshurst. Lord Leicester, who along with Henry had joined the royalist cause, had sent a messenger from the battlefield. He had told the messenger to deliver a letter to a member of the household staff, a man called Sudbury, who was to break the news to Dorothy's mother, Lady Leicester, rather than Dorothy. But Dorothy saw the messenger arriving and the very fact that he asked to see Sudbury put her on the alert.

She waylaid Sudbury and insisted on knowing what the message was. He tried saying only that he thought Henry's friend Lord Falkland had been killed, but Dorothy knew there was something more. Finally he admitted that Henry had been wounded, but held back on telling her the whole awful truth. "This put her into a great passion of grief," he wrote apologetically to his employer. "Her grief, I perceived, was the greater because she feared I had not told her all."

Sudbury managed to slip away from Dorothy and get to the anxious Lady Leicester, who fainted as soon as she heard the news that her son-in-law was dead. When she recovered, Sudbury persuaded her to "put on all possible courage and resolution, and to go and comfort my Lady Sunderland". He added in his letter to Lord Leicester, "I shall not need to tell your Lordship that neither of their Ladyships took much rest that night."

Dorothy's grief was so all-consuming her family was afraid for her life. Finally her father wrote to her, sympathising with her loss but urging her to be strong. "Besides the vanity of bemoaning that which hath no remedy, you offend him whom you loved if you hurt that person whom he loved. Remember how apprehensive he was of your dangers, and how sorry for any thing that troubled you. Imagine how he sees that you afflict and hurt yourself."

Her father's kind but stern words struck home and Dorothy pulled herself together. Her baby was born but did not survive to infancy. To protect her children she stayed at Penshurst, but planned to return to the Spencer estates as soon as she could. However, the Parliamentarians had sacked Althorp and the Royalists razed the mansion at Wormleighton to keep it from being used as a Roundhead stronghold.

When the conflict finally ended, the Roundheads emerged victorious and the repercussions for those who had opposed them began in earnest. Early in 1649, the enemies of the defeated King Charles I put him on trial and condemned him to death. He was beheaded on a scaffold set up in front of the banqueting hall at Whitehall Palace. Parliament subsequently passed an act abolishing the monarchy.

During the Commonwealth that followed the war, the victors, led by the Puritan Oliver Cromwell, sequestered the Spencer estates. Dorothy could have thrown up her hands in despair and stayed at Penshurst with her loving family, living in easy luxury and letting others take care of her and her children. Instead, she began directing repairs to the Spencer estates. She enlisted the help of her brothers and Henry's Puritan uncle, Edward Spencer, to have the confiscated lands released without the usual heavy fines. When their efforts succeeded, she set to work organising repairs to Althorp.

Without Dorothy's unwavering determination, the Althorp estate, if it had survived at all, would not have remained in the Spencer family. The work of generations of Spencers would have been forgotten – and it is unlikely that Diana Spencer would have become Princess of Wales.

Dorothy made improvements to the manor house, having the inner courtyard roofed over and building a grand staircase. This elegant structure is considered the most striking feature of the mansion today. She replanted the gardens and made Althorp a home again. In 1651, Dorothy and her children finally moved back to Althorp for good. Her son Robert, second Earl of Sunderland, was 11 years old.

Determined to give her son a gentleman's education, Dorothy arranged for first-rate schooling. When Robert was 17, she sent him on a tour of France, Italy and Spain. Accompanied by an Oxford don and another of her brothers, Henry Sidney – Robert's same-age uncle – the young earl set off for his first great adventure. Lord Leicester supplied letters of introduction to members of Europe's nobility, giving the young men access to their grand homes and glittering society. Robert polished his French and Spanish, practising the latter when he went on to Spain on his own. By the time he returned home three years later he'd acquired a love for all things European, expensive taste in art and furnishings, and a familiarity with the languages and courts of the Continent.

Robert arrived back in England just before the restoration of the monarchy in May 1660. He was now equipped with everything his father would have wanted him to have – except a sense of honour. The long, bitter war and the punishing years afterwards had left a mark on Henry Spencer's son that even Dorothy couldn't erase. He had seen up close the dubious rewards of honour.

Chapter 2
The Courtesans

hen Charles II returned to England to take his place on the throne, the generation that had come of age in a time of strict Puritan rule was ready to break loose. Embittered by years of suffering and deprivation, they were cynical, acquisitive pleasure-seekers. And Charles himself set the tone.

Self-indulgence in Charles II's court became even more frantic after the bubonic plague hit London again in 1665, claiming more than 100,000 victims. No sooner had the piled-up carts bearing the dead to common graves stopped trundling through the streets, than the Great Fire broke out and spread with unholy speed to destroy huge sections of the city. The king was personally heroic during the fire; he even helped battle the flames. But soon afterwards, he resumed his live-hard, die-young attitude with more abandon than ever. On the day an edict against drunkenness was issued, he drank himself silly.

If Diana Spencer could have travelled back in time and visited the court of King Charles II, she might have thought she'd stumbled into a Spencer family reunion. Besides the king himself, numerous courtiers and mistresses were Diana's forebears.

Charles kept many mistresses, 13 of them known to history by name. He acknowledged 14 of their respective offspring and was reported to have sired many others he didn't acknowledge or even know about.

At least three of the king's most famous courtesans were Diana Spencer's direct ancestors. One of them wasn't at the court, having died just before Charles regained his throne. The other two were well ensconced at Whitehall Palace and wielded far more power as mistresses than Charles's wife could ever dream of.

"Beautiful Strumpet"

Charles Stuart and Lucy Walters met in the summer of 1648, when they were both about 18 years old. They were living in The Hague, both exiles. His father was still alive but the defeated king's days were numbered.

During the Civil War Lucy had been forced to flee her home, Roch Castle in Wales, when the Roundheads burned it down as punishment for her father's support of the king.

She'd made her way to London, then across the Channel to The Netherlands.

Claims were made that Lucy and Charles married each other in secret around this time. Charles denied it all his life, although he acknowledged her son as his and named him James Scott. Charles never denied paternity, even when James grew up bearing a distinct resemblance to handsome Robert Sidney, one of Lucy's other alleged protectors. However, Charles never bestowed legitimacy and a right to succeed to the throne on the young man.

A diarist of the era dismissed Lucy as "a most beautiful strumpet" and "an insipid creature", but she seems to have been important to Charles for some time. Their on/off relationship lasted until he left for Scotland in 1651 to reclaim his crown and mount an invasion of England.

The invasion failed and Charles's army was trounced by Oliver Cromwell's troops at the Battle of Worcester. The would-be king of England escaped capture by hiding in a large oak tree. He then disguised himself as best he could and made his way to the coast with the help of a royalist underground. His powerful charisma, six-foot-four physique and the Mediterranean colouring of his Medici heritage made it tricky for Charles to fade into the background. The harrowing adventure took six weeks and several close shaves before he finally boarded a boat to the Continent.

When he reached The Hague and learned that Lucy had taken up with another man, reputedly Henry Bennett, Earl of Arlington, Charles cut off contact with her. A few months later she gave birth to a little girl named Mary. Two of Mary's descendants found their way into the Spencer line, making Lucy Walters Diana's nine times great-grandmother from more than one direction.

Lucy's damaged reputation had made life difficult for her at The Hague, so she decided to return to England with her children. Knowing a propaganda tool when he saw one, Oliver Cromwell had Lucy arrested, describing her as a "wife or mistress" of the former Prince of Wales. In Puritan England the word "mistress" in that context was censure enough.

Lucy spent two weeks in prison being interrogated before Cromwell released her in a blaze of publicity, milking her sinful past for all it was worth. He crowed that this was the kind of woman Charles Stuart spent money on, which proved what kind of profligate and immoral sovereign he would have been if he hadn't been chased out of the country. This allegation, of course, turned out to be quite true.

Cromwell's officers then took Lucy and her children to Flanders and dumped them ashore. Left to make her way as best she could, she headed for Brussels.

By this time Charles had heard troubling reports about Lucy's lifestyle and decided to send an agent to spy on her. The resulting report suggested that young James was being neglected and that his mother was little better than a prostitute living in squalor, so Charles made up his mind to take the boy from her.

Lucy didn't give up James without a fight. Only after embarrassing public scenes, an exchange of threats and the use of powerful connections did Charles manage to defeat his former beloved. Charles placed the boy in the care of Baron William Crofts. Lucy's son went by the name of James Crofts and was sent to school in Paris in 1658 to fill in the gaps in his education. Lucy followed her boy to Paris as soon as she could, but passed away shortly after arriving. Not surprisingly, history claims she died of a venereal disease.

After Charles regained his throne in 1660, James went to live at his father's court. In 1663 the king gave his son a title, Duke of Monmouth, then married him to the heiress Lady Anne Scott, Countess of Buccleuch in her own right. Among the additional titles they received as a couple was the Dukedom of Buccleuch.

James took the recognition to heart and felt he deserved to succeed his father to the throne, so he revived the story of his parents' secret elopement. Supposedly a certificate of marriage was hidden away in some mysterious black box, but the box was never located and James's tale remained suspect.

Two centuries later, James's descendant, the fifth Duke of Buccleuch, allegedly found among his papers the crucial certificate proving that Charles II had married Lucy Walters. Word has it that he gave the certificate to Queen Victoria. She thanked him, then promptly burned it.

"For Old Times' Sake"

Barbara Palmer, born Barbara Villiers, was the most charismatic, demanding and widely despised of the king's concubines. She had joined his court-in-exile in The Netherlands and was ensconced as his mistress from the beginning of the Restoration in 1660.

Barbara had been left in straitened circumstances when her royalist father, a viscount, died from a battle wound. Although she was a great beauty, her lack of a dowry had spoiled her chances for the kind of marriage she should have been able to expect. But she had more than enough spirit to compensate.

A romance with the Earl of Chesterfield had fizzled because he was looking for a rich wife. So Barbara settled for Roger Palmer, who married her against his family's wishes. She took up with the future king right after her marriage and gave birth to a child who could have been fathered by her husband, by Charles or by the Earl of Chesterfield. Palmer had his suspicions but did not make a fuss. His complaisance earned him the titles Baron of Limerick and Earl of Castlemaine, which must have been some consolation. Barbara became Countess of Castlemaine.

When Barbara and her husband parted company, she was pregnant again. This time there was no doubt in anyone's mind of the father's identity. Barbara was clearly the king's favourite.

Around this time, Charles decided he should get married, choosing the Portuguese Catherine of Braganza (known as the Infanta) for the huge dowry she could bring to his coffers. Catherine was Catholic so the marriage was unpopular with the king's subjects. The marriage didn't go over very well with Barbara, either.

Charles was the epitome of charm and gallantry when he met Catherine at Portsmouth to welcome her to her new home. They were married in May 1662 in two ceremonies, first in a secret Roman Catholic service for the bride's sake, then with very public Anglican rites to please the people of England. The innocent Catherine fell hopelessly in love with her sexy, experienced husband and they were happy together for all of a few weeks.

Everything changed when Barbara gave birth to a boy. After she and her husband had split up, Barbara became totally dependent on Charles and begged him not to abandon her.

In a scenario that seems eerily similar to the 20th-century Charles–Diana–Camilla triangle, the king's relationship with Barbara took up where it had left off – and the queen was expected to be a good sport about it. But Charles crossed the line when he appointed Barbara as his bride's Lady of the Bedchamber and formally presented her to the queen. The entire court was shocked. The queen was so upset she got a nosebleed and fainted.

Charles sent his chief adviser to Catherine to urge her not to take his infidelity personally. It was merely a royal privilege, the adviser explained, a tradition recognised by the very best families throughout Europe – including the queen's own father.

Catherine, having very little choice in the matter, learned to accept the situation. Barbara wasn't as accommodating when Charles strayed, as he tended to do quite often. She had a violent temper and the quarrels that erupted in her quarters were ferocious, much like the alleged explosions between Diana and her Charles.

During Barbara's next pregnancy in 1667, the king accused her of having had an affair and told her he didn't intend to recognise the child as his. Barbara reportedly swore that if Charles denied paternity of the baby she would "bring it into Whitehall and dash the brains of it out before the King's face".

Charles was understandably horrified by Barbara's threat. Before she was through with him, he was on his knees begging forgiveness for his ugly, unfounded suspicions. Actually, the suspicions had been very well-founded. Barbara had a whole stable of lovers.

Whether or not all the children Barbara bore while she was involved with Charles were his offspring, most received the name Fitzroy, derived from *fils du roi*, meaning sons of the king. Henry Fitzroy, the second son, was made Earl of Euston and Duke of Grafton. Five generations later one of his descendants married Frederick Spencer, Diana's great-great-great-grandfather.

The level of Barbara's influence over the king varied through the years, depending on how capricious her behaviour was and whether Charles was in love with someone else. In 1670 he awarded Barbara property and several new titles, including Duchess of Cleveland. No one seemed sure whether the honours were a goodbye gift or an indication that she was back in favour, though he did acknowledge the child she was carrying as his. "You may tell the Duchess of Cleveland", he is quoted as saying, "that I know the child is not mine, yet I will acknowledge it for old times' sake."

But Barbara was about to be bumped.

"Mrs. Carwell"

Louise de Kerouaille was a lady-in-waiting to the Duchess of Orleans, Charles's youngest and favourite sister, Henriette Anne. In 1670 the duchess's brother-in-law, King Louis XIV of France, sent her to England along with a battalion of diplomats. Louis hoped the duchess could use her influence over her brother to help forge a new Anglo-French alliance.

When Charles met his sister at Dover, he was quick to notice her new lady-in-waiting. After one look at the lustrous dark hair, almond-shaped eyes and sensual lips of the lovely French 20-year-old, he decided he had to have her. Louise's soft, carefully modulated voice, coupled with the refined manners she'd perfected by studying the most sophisticated ladies of the French court, appealed to him. She was a delightful contrast to the strident Barbara.

But Charles's sister took her responsibility to her young ladies and their parents seriously. Aware of her brother's dishonourable intentions, Henriette Anne took Louise with her when she returned to France. The duchess was ill, however, and died just a few weeks later. Mademoiselle de Kerouaille was left without a protector.

Louis XIV promptly arranged to send Louise back to England on a royal yacht, hoping to curry favour with Charles and use Louise as a pillow-talk spy. Louise was the product of a noble but impoverished family and was determined to improve her prospects. Her gentleness comforted Charles in his grief over his sister, and eventually he decided she should be given the post of maid of honour to his wife. The queen, presumably, had given up on making a fuss about that sort of arrangement by this time.

The Duke of Buckingham, who was one of the king's advisers, filled Louise's head with dreams of glory. He told her the royal marriage would be over soon and Charles would be looking for another wife. Perhaps Buckingham was lying, or perhaps he was genuinely hoping Charles would divorce Catherine for failing to give him an heir. Whatever the case, the king wouldn't hear of setting his wife aside. All evidence to the contrary, he was much too fond of her.

But Louise believed Buckingham and decided to try for a crown, opting for the classic ploy of playing hard to get. Charles was so infatuated with her that she got away with her demure flirtation for months.

Lady Arlington, the wife of another of the king's inner circle of ministers, bluntly told Louise she'd better decide whether she wanted to be a royal mistress or end up as a nun. Then the lady consulted with the French ambassador, whose masters were beginning to worry that Louise was being too coy and would end up losing the king's interest. The two schemers came up with a plan to help things along a little.

Charles was planning to attend the races at Newmarket near the Arlington mansion, so it was natural for Lord and Lady Arlington to entertain him while he was there. Lady Arlington invited the French ambassador as well, adding that she would be delighted if he brought Louise along. Charles was especially attentive to Louise at the dinner party, and she was at her eyelash-batting best.

Lady Arlington playfully suggested that since they were in the country, they should hold a mock rustic wedding. The king would play the groom and Louise would be the innocent bride.

Louise hesitated, but gave in. A bedroom was prepared and she was laid on the bed, her clothing loosened in charming disarray. The audience laughed as if they were all just sharing an innocent joke, but abruptly withdrew when the "groom" arrived and climbed into the bed.

By morning the "bride" was the king's mistress and nine months later gave birth to a son. As soon as she had settled in as the new royal favourite and understood that she probably wouldn't replace the queen, Louise began making the most of her opportunity.

She had a gift for wheedling goodies out of the king by using babyish coaxing or, if that failed, buckets of tears. In due time she was enjoying 40 rooms for her private use in Whitehall Palace, along with a seemingly unlimited decorating budget. Charles heaped jewellery and other lavish gifts on her and she received a generous annual pension and opportunities to make even more money by various means, such as selling licences to merchants. Poverty was behind her at last, but she always needed money. She had picked up the habit of gambling and was more daring than lucky.

Because she was French and Catholic, the English public didn't like Louise, calling her "Mrs. Carwell", their Anglicised version of her Gallic last name. An unfriendly mob once jeered at the gilded carriage they thought was hers, only to switch to uproarious laughter when the king's more popular mistress, the Drury Lane actress Nell Gwynn, stuck her head out the window and shouted, "Be silent, good people! I am the Protestant whore!"

In 1673, the king awarded his "dearest Fubbs", as he affectionately called Louise, the title of Duchess of Portsmouth. Two years later he asked Robert Spencer, the Earl of Sunderland (Diana's seven times great-grandfather), to handle the negotiations to settle the title of Duke of Richmond on their year-old child, Charles Lennox. This Charles produced a line of progeny that included Diana's maternal grandmother.

The Courtesans

With women such as Lucy, Barbara and Louise in her background, it is little wonder Diana was not willing to settle for the narrow role of producing heirs and doing whatever she was told. And these three strong women were purring kittens compared to the roaring lioness about to make her entrance onto the Spencer family stage.

Chapter 3
The Golden Girl

In the long saga of British history, there is no one else quite like Sarah Churchill, Duchess of Marlborough. Beautiful, strong-willed and controversial, Sarah played out her life on a grand scale against a backdrop of seismic events. Her most famous descendant, Princess Diana, gave the British monarchy a bit of a shaking-up, but Sarah helped pull the throne right out from under a king of her era.

Sarah was a self-made woman in a male-dominated society. She began her life in genteel poverty and ended it as the wealthiest woman in Britain, not by finding a rich husband but by making her husband rich. Not only did she control his finances, she amassed a separate fortune in her own right.

As ambitious for her family as for herself, Sarah saw to it that three of her daughters became duchesses and one a countess, and largely through her efforts her granddaughters hooked up with five dukes and two earls.

When Sarah arranged for the marriage of her favourite daughter to a Spencer, she set in motion a series of events that led to the creation of two separate Spencer dynasties. One produced Diana, Princess of Wales. From the other line came Sir Winston Spencer Churchill, the prime minister of Britain who attained legendary status by guiding his country to victory through the bleak years of World War II.

In her private life, most of Sarah's personal and family relationships were stormy. In the public arena, Sarah had to play down the importance of her influence or risk criticism for poking her pretty nose into men's affairs. Her frustration shows in one of her more poignant comments: "I am confident I should have been the greatest hero that ever was known in the Parliament House, if I had been so happy to have been a man."

Perhaps she was right, but even so, not many men could boast of as many accomplishments as Sarah racked up during her lifetime.

Bewitched, Bothered and Bewildered

Sarah Jennings burst onto an unsuspecting world at St Albans in Hertfordshire on 5 June 1660, a week after Charles II's triumphant return to London as England's monarch.

The Jennings family didn't live in poverty, but they were in constant debt from struggling to keep up appearances as minor gentry. When Sarah was eight her father died and her mother, Frances, packed up her daughters and moved to London. As the daughter of a baron, Frances Jennings was given quarters in St James's Palace, the official royal home of the king's brother, James, the Duke of York.

Sarah's older sister, also named Frances, became a maid of honour to the first Duchess of York, the former Anne Hyde – who was the last English woman to marry an heir to the British throne until Diana Spencer married the Prince of Wales in 1981.

Although the pay for a maid of honour was negligible, the job came with the promise of a dowry from the crown. This bonus enhanced a young lady's chances of marrying well if she was smart enough not to be seduced by a courtier, only to find herself pregnant and discarded. Frances, "la belle Jennings", was smart enough, and soon married a lord.

When the first Duchess of York died in 1671, she left only two surviving daughters, Lady Mary and Lady Anne. Both had been raised as Protestants by order of King Charles. The duke remarried in 1673, choosing the 15-year-old Mary Beatrice of Modena, a staunch Catholic. Sarah, who was now 13, landed a position as the new duchess's maid of honour.

Vivacious, confident Sarah, with her sparkling blue eyes and a cloud of strawberry blonde hair setting off her creamy skin and attractive features, was four years older than Lady

Anne. She simply dazzled the mousy little girl with the perpetual squinting frown. Anne developed a case of heroine worship that would last almost three decades.

Later, Sarah also caught the attention of several court rakes, including John Churchill. John was 25 years old, 10 years older than Sarah. He'd started as a page in the duke's household, but had chalked up an impressive military record since then. He'd seen action in naval engagements in the Mediterranean and distinguished himself in land battles in the Anglo-Dutch wars.

In 1675, John was back at St James's Palace serving the Duke of York in key court posts. Tall, handsome and well-mannered, John Churchill cut a dashing figure at court – perhaps too dashing; he had an affair with Barbara Castlemaine while she was still the king's mistress. When he turned his charm on 15-year-old Sarah, everyone expected her to swoon right into his waiting arms.

But John was precisely the kind of man Sarah was most leery of, and she made him jump through hoops to prove that his intentions were honourable. Despite opposition from John's parents, who had wanted him to wed an heiress, they married when Sarah was 17.

The couple enjoyed precious little time together as husband and wife before the Duke of York sent John on a mission to Brussels. The duke had noticed over the years that the young man, recently made a colonel, possessed exceptional diplomatic skills, so John was appointed to a special delegation negotiating a new alliance between England and France. Sarah remained at court for a while, then moved in with John's parents in Dorset – a situation that did nothing to improve her thorny relationship with her in-laws.

John inundated her with love letters and sent her a beautiful ring, but felt he wasn't receiving much affection in return. "I find you are not of the same mind", he commented in a note, "for when you write you are afraid to tell me that you love me."

Stuck in the country with his family, Sarah probably didn't feel particularly loving at that juncture. In any case, she would always be the pragmatic spouse, leaving the hearts and flowers to her adoring husband.

And despite her utter devotion to him, Sarah would keep John Churchill slightly off balance on the home front for the rest of his life.

Secrets, Lies and Treachery

Word had spread throughout England that the Duke of York, influenced by his Catholic wife, was turning increasingly to the Church of Rome. The rumours set off a wave of anti-papist hysteria throughout the country. The king, who was fond of his brother, ordered the duke to take an extended vacation somewhere out of sight until the nation calmed down. The York household packed their bags and went to Brussels. John and Sarah Churchill joined them there in August 1679, even though Sarah was pregnant.

When the household returned to London temporarily before going on to Scotland, Sarah chose to remain in London to have her baby. John had to accompany the duke and then travel back to the Continent several times to handle various diplomatic missions on the duke's behalf, so she stayed alone at John's former bachelor quarters. During this time, John was recommended for positions such as English minister at The Hague or ambassador to Paris, but the duke wanted to retain his services. John had to put his personal ambitions on hold.

Sarah's baby, a little girl they named Harriot, was born in January 1680. John was unable to be there for the birth, and had to be content with writing to Sarah to express his joy. By the time John finally came home in March, little Harriot had died. After the delight they'd felt at her birth, both parents must have found the loss hard to bear.

John spent the next year travelling between London and Edinburgh, but when Sarah produced a second daughter, Henrietta, he was there for the child's christening in July 1681.

Two months later, Sarah's leave of absence from the York household came to an end. She was still a working woman, and her wages for attending the Duchess of York and Lady Anne – who were still in Scotland – were important to the Churchills. Faced with the eternal tug-of-war between career and motherhood, 21-year-old Sarah chose the option – not uncommon at that time – of entrusting her baby to servants and relatives while she returned to her job.

While in Edinburgh, the Duke of York tried to stamp out Presbyterianism by encouraging the persecution of its adherents. Sarah witnessed some grisly executions and was horrified, though at that stage of her career she kept her feelings to herself.

In 1682, the duke rewarded John for his loyal service by giving him a Scottish barony. That same year, King Charles gave his permission for the York household to return to London.

With their combined salaries providing a comfortable income, John and Sarah began sprucing up their London lodgings. Sarah bought out her sister's share in their St Albans home, and the Churchills started making renovations there.

When the younger York daughter, Lady Anne, married Prince George of Denmark, the couple set up their own household in "the Cockpit" – a building adjoining the king's court at Whitehall Palace. Anne asked her father for permission to have Sarah Churchill transferred from her stepmother's service to hers. Some of the duke's advisers warned him against such a move. Sarah was known to favour Whigs, the politicians who promoted the supremacy of parliament over the royal prerogative. The advisers were concerned that she could be a bad influence on the impressionable Anne.

Nevertheless, the duke granted his daughter's request, and Sarah switched from Mary Beatrice's household to Anne's.

Sarah seems to have been fond of Anne in their early days together and was particularly sympathetic to her struggle to have children. Anne's pregnancies – at least 17 in all – resulted in miscarriages and infant deaths in every instance except one. Herself a mother, Sarah was able to offer comfort and practical advice to the younger woman, and Anne grew increasingly dependent on her. When Sarah and John had a second daughter in 1684, they named her Anne in honour of Sarah's mistress.

In February 1685, King Charles II collapsed with a seizure and died five days later. Since Charles had left no legitimate children, the Duke of York took his place on the throne as King James II and moved his household to Whitehall. The new king appointed John Churchill to an important position with a salary increase, then raised him to the English peerage as Baron Churchill.

John proved his mettle as a defender of the crown when the late King Charles's illegitimate son, the Duke of Monmouth – who was a Protestant and insisted he was legitimate – landed in England in a bid to take the throne by force from his uncle. Appointed major-general of the king's troops, John put down the rebellion and easily routed the rebels. Monmouth was captured and later beheaded. Punitive action taken against his supporters, called the "Bloody Assizes", severely damaged the monarch's popularity. He made matters worse when he dissolved parliament.

In 1686, the Churchills finally had a son and named him

John after his father. The future looked bright except for the widespread erosion of trust in King James. He had launched a campaign to strengthen the authority of the monarchy and secure religious tolerance for minorities, especially Catholics. His critics interpreted his actions as steps towards royal tyranny and a return to official Catholicism.

In 1687, Sarah gave birth to another daughter, Elizabeth, but her growing family didn't get in the way of her involvement in politics. Vividly recalling the persecution she'd seen in Scotland, and angered by the king's high-handed ways, Sarah embraced the opinion taking hold in the country that he should be deposed on the grounds of his Catholicism and replaced by a Protestant monarch.

The logical choice was his daughter, Princess Mary, who had been raised in the Church of England and was married to another Protestant, Prince William of Orange. William was the Stadholder of the Dutch Republic and the couple lived at The Hague.

Princess Anne took up her sister's cause. Probably she was under the influence of Sarah, just as the king's advisers had predicted. But it couldn't have escaped Anne that she herself would be heir to the throne if Mary became queen and produced no children to succeed her.

Princess Anne communicated regularly and in secret with her sister to keep her updated on events in England. The news that caused the greatest alarm was that King James's wife, Queen Mary Beatrice, was pregnant again. She had not yet managed to produce a healthy boy, but if she did, he would leapfrog over both his half-sisters as heir to the throne – even though he would be Catholic. Family ties and the friendships forged in their youth at St James's Palace were forgotten as Anne claimed that her stepmother was perpetrating a hoax. The queen, Anne insisted, was stuffing a cushion under her dress to fake a pregnancy.

Pamphleteers grabbed the story and ran with it, subjecting the queen to an orgy of slander. When she confounded the gossips by bearing a son in June 1688, a new tale was concocted. The child was said to be a changeling, smuggled into her chamber in a warming pan. The fact that the birth had been properly witnessed by a roomful of courtiers, both Catholic and Protestant, didn't seem to dispel the lies.

A group of powerful men – later known as the "Immortal Seven" – drafted a letter inviting William of Orange to England to "give assistance" under the current circumstances.

When word arrived in London that William had begun an intense military and naval build-up in The Netherlands, Princess Anne and Sarah Churchill hatched a scheme of their own. Sarah acted as go-between, arranging for help for herself and the princess from members of the Immortal Seven in the event of a crisis.

The crisis came soon enough. William landed in England with his troops in November 1688 and marched toward London. He was careful to claim he had come only to protect the liberties of the English people.

The End of a Monarchy

King James headed for Salisbury Plain on 18 November to join his troops. Many of the royalist officers were more interested in joining William than fighting him, and by this time Baron John Churchill was also leaning in that direction.

The king held a council of war on 23 November 1688 to determine whether the army should advance or retreat. He seemed incapable of reaching a firm decision, and his dithering was the last straw for John. When the council ended, John and two other commanders quietly rode with their men towards William's camp to join the invasion troops. Princess Anne's husband followed suit shortly afterwards.

John had left a letter of apology for James. It was filled with excuses and self-justifications for his defection, and claimed he'd gone only because his country and his religion were in peril.

King James retaliated by sending an order to London for the seizure of Churchill's possessions. He also issued a warrant for the arrest of Princess Anne's two ladies-in-waiting – Sarah and the wife of one of the other deserters. Until the warrant could be served, guards were to be posted outside Princess Anne's quarters.

But the three women and a female servant escaped from the building by a secret staircase. Aided by members of the Anglican clergy and the lords conspiring against King James, they made it safely to Nottingham.

Early the next morning, the arrest order for Sarah

reached London, and the king arrived a little later. Still unaware that Princess Anne had turned against him, he was certain she was as shattered as he was by the treachery all around them. When he discovered that she too had abandoned him and was supporting William and Mary's bid for the throne, he cried, "God help me. Even my daughters have deserted me."

Realising he had been beaten, King James decided to spirit his family out of England. His wife fled with their son to France, where she was taken under the protective wing of James's cousin, King Louis XIV. James joined them there later, after narrowly escaping capture by his enemies.

James never set foot in England again. He didn't abdicate officially, but in late January 1689 parliament decided that his flight to France amounted to an abdication. After much debate, it was decided that William and Mary would rule together until one of them died. The survivor would continue on the throne, and Princess Anne would be next in line.

Anne was hesitant. William as consort was one thing; William as king was another. However, Sarah successfully urged her not to contest the co-monarchy. When William was told of Sarah's efforts, he was offended rather than grateful, annoyed that she had so much influence over his sister-in-law.

Sarah's next lobbying effort angered him even more. He had offered Princess Anne a pension from the Privy Purse, but Sarah pushed for an annual grant from parliament for

Anne that would make her independent of the king and queen for revenue.

Princess Anne received her parliamentary grant and was generous in showing her gratitude to Sarah for pushing the issue. But a rift had opened up in the royal family, and William and Mary blamed Sarah. In a new reign, the acrimony didn't make for an auspicious beginning.

The Tainted Fruits of Victory

As soon as he was king, William declared war on France. He now had England's armies at his disposal for the ongoing conflict between France and the coalition of his allies in Europe. He gave John Churchill the title of Earl of Marlborough and placed him at the head of the English troops in the coalition. Sent to Flanders with a command of 8000 troops, the new earl won successive victories over the French.

Sarah gave birth to a fourth daughter. The Churchills, now known as the Marlboroughs, named the child Mary in honour of Queen Mary. In 1690, Marlborough was back at home when the couple had a second son, Charles. Their family now consisted of six children, four girls and two boys. A future Marlborough dynasty seemed to be guaranteed.

A week after the boy's birth, Marlborough joined King William in Ireland to help fight the Jacobites, the supporters of the deposed King James, who were being backed by France. Marlborough's military skills helped to assure William's ultimate victory, but the rewards and honours he had expected didn't come his way. He complained loudly when he saw the best available positions go to the king's Dutch friends.

King William grew tired of Marlborough's grumbling and was fed up with the discord between the queen and Princess Anne – for which he blamed Marlborough's wife. The royal sisters were feuding because Mary had repeatedly ordered Anne to dismiss Sarah, and Anne had repeatedly refused. In January 1692, the king suddenly stripped Marlborough of his posts, probably for stirring up resistance against the promotion of foreigners in the English army and the peerage.

The worst moment for Marlborough came in early May 1692, when he was arrested and taken to the Tower of London. The charge was high treason. He was the victim of a trumped-up story and the key evidence against him was a forged document, but he spent six weeks in the Tower.

Sarah, deeply afraid that he would end up on the scaffold, was allowed only two visits with her husband in all that time. To make this dismal situation worse, their two-year-old son fell ill. During her second visit, Sarah had to tell Marlborough that their little boy had died. John was 42, Sarah 32, and they must have felt as if their lives were falling apart.

Marlborough was finally released on bail and in mid-June his case was heard at the King's Bench. He easily proved his innocence, but when the hearing ended, he and Sarah wanted only to go home to Holywell House and grieve for their child in private.

They could have had no inkling at that low ebb in their

fortunes that their greatest triumphs were still ahead.

The Marital Merger

Robert Spencer of Althorp, second Earl of Sunderland (known as Sunderland), had managed to make himself an indispensable adviser to King Charles II, then to King James II, only to fall out of favour with both monarchs. Blatantly opportunistic, the man who has been referred to as "Shameless Sunderland" was a brilliant manipulator of other ambitious men. His weakness for collecting art and beautiful objects, coupled with a serious addiction to gambling, left him constantly strapped for money.

After James II had lost his throne, Sunderland had headed for The Netherlands, accompanied by his family. But he had been making a gradual comeback since 1688. It seemed he simply knew too much about handling difficult politicians and managing elections to be left out in the cold forever. In 1692, the same year that saw John and Sarah Marlborough hit rock bottom, Sunderland returned to live at his beloved Althorp and take his seat in the House of Lords.

In September of that year, Sarah resumed her post with Princess Anne at Berkeley House in Piccadilly, where Anne and her husband were now living. Their ongoing quarrel with the monarchs escalated until Sarah offered to leave Anne's household to appease the queen. When Anne begged her not to go, Sarah stayed on.

The one bright spot in the midst of the turmoil was

that Princess Anne gave birth at last to a son who survived the crucial first weeks of life. Since William and Mary had no children of their own and seemed to have given up hope of having any, Anne's success in providing an eventual heir enhanced her position considerably. Yet the sisters' feuding continued, ending in a terrible quarrel that was never resolved between them.

Queen Mary died of smallpox in 1694 and William, having treated her with harsh condescension throughout their life together, suddenly realised how much she'd meant to him. He proceeded to fall apart, drinking heavily.

Sunderland advised Princess Anne to write a letter of condolence to her brother-in-law, and although she'd always loathed the oily earl she listened to him. Sarah was against the idea, but for once Princess Anne ignored her. Although the royal rapprochement was mainly for show and the two in-laws continued to despise each other, they put up a united front, and William gave up trying to pry Sarah loose from Anne's household.

Peace was restored to Europe in the autumn of 1697. Like Sunderland, Marlborough had inched his way back into favour and by 1698 had regained his old army rank, as well as his position on Privy Council.

The eldest of Sarah's three daughters, Henrietta, had married the son of their friend Sidney Godolphin, and Princess Anne had contributed £5000 towards her dowry. The princess was prepared to do the same for Sarah's younger girls.

The Earl of Sunderland's son, Charles Spencer, was a widower, still mourning his late first wife, who had died within a year of their wedding. Nevertheless, his mother waited barely a month after her daughter-in-law's funeral to approach Sarah about the possibility of a match between her son and Sarah's second-oldest daughter, Anne.

Sarah liked the idea, but her husband was against it. Charles Spencer struck Marlborough as a rough sort of man. Tall and plain-looking, his complexion badly scarred by smallpox, Charles seemed more interested in books than people and was reputed to be hot-tempered, rude and a self-important radical bent on eradicating the peerage.

Charles himself was in no hurry to remarry and resisted meeting Anne Churchill when his mother suggested it. But the first time he saw the young woman, he changed his tune. She had inherited her mother's beauty and her father's winning personality, and Charles fell instantly in love with her.

Since Anne seemed just as taken with Charles, her father gave his consent and the wedding plans proceeded. Princess Anne made the promised contribution to the bridal dowry of her namesake, and the couple married at the beginning of 1699.

Their union would reconfigure the future Spencer family in ways no one could ever have anticipated.

Fickle Fortune
As the century drew to a close, Europe was moving towards

war again. William was gravely ill and knew that Princess Anne would soon be queen. He could see that the Earl of Marlborough, as the husband of Princess Anne's most trusted confidante, would be the most powerful man in her government. Bowing to the inevitable, the king made Marlborough commander-in-chief of the English forces in The Netherlands and arranged for the earl to succeed him as leader of the coalition against France.

In July 1700, Princess Anne's only surviving child died. His mother would never fully recover from the tragedy, and the obesity and arthritis already plaguing her would worsen until she was an invalid before she was 40. Suddenly, the English line of succession was of urgent interest throughout the country and in Europe.

William gave his assent to the Act of Settlement in June 1701, which stipulated that Princess Anne's heir would be Sophie of Hanover, a Protestant granddaughter of James I.

Marlborough and the king sailed to The Hague a month later, but William moved on to a palace retreat and left the earl with the inherently contradictory task of trying to preserve an uneasy peace while organising a new Grand Alliance for war.

In mid-September, the deposed King James died. Louis XIV unexpectedly, and against the counsel of all his advisers, recognised James II's son, also named James, as King of England, Ireland and Scotland. The gesture meant little in real terms, but it created an unpleasant diplomatic incident.

William immediately expelled the French ambassador and recalled the English ambassador from Paris. If the English people's support for war had been declining, it suddenly spiked.

In February 1702, King William was riding his horse when it stumbled on a molehill and threw him, leaving him with a broken collarbone and, more dangerously, pneumonia. He died in March 1702 at the age of 52.

Much to Sarah's satisfaction, Princess Anne became queen and immediately began handing out honours to her friends. She made Marlborough a Knight of the Garter and appointed him Captain General of the country's military forces and Master-General of the Ordnance, honours he'd coveted for years.

Sarah received several top-level appointments, including Ranger of Windsor Park, which came with a beautiful house within the Windsor Castle grounds. Her married daughters were appointed Ladies of the Bedchamber at generous salaries, and Marlborough's younger brothers won key positions. At Sarah's urging, Marlborough lobbied the queen to make Sydney Godolphin Lord Treasurer, a position equivalent to today's prime minister.

In May 1702, two months after Anne had inherited the throne, England and her allies declared war on France. The Earl of Marlborough set out on another mission to the Continent as commander of the forces.

By the end of the campaign, the allies had reduced the number and strength of the French fortresses in The

Netherlands, and Marlborough was hailed as a hero. He returned to The Hague to streets filled with cheering crowds, and in November went home to England to accept his grateful queen's offer of a dukedom, the most exalted title in the kingdom. Sarah Jennings Churchill, now the Duchess of Marlborough, had come a very long way.

In the meantime, Charles Spencer had become the third Earl of Sunderland on the death of his father and was now known as Sunderland. He had annoyed both Sarah and the queen by criticising the pension paid to Queen Anne's consort and questioning the very existence of the monarchy.

But domestic squabbles faded into unimportance when Sarah learned that John, her only remaining son, was ill. He was 16 years old and studying at Cambridge, where he had contracted a particularly severe strain of smallpox. When Sarah heard the news, her first fear was that her handsome son's skin could be pitted with scars. Once she'd rushed to his bedside, she realised that scars were the least of her worries.

Marlborough wrote to Sarah, begging her to keep him apprised of the situation, and the anguished helplessness of a desperate parent shows in every line. "If you think anything under heaven can be done, pray let me know it. Or if you think my coming can be of least use let me know it. I beg I may hear as soon as possible, for I have no thought but what is at Cambridge."

As hope faded, Sarah sent for her husband and he rushed to her side. Their son died on 20 February 1703, and the couple immediately left for St Albans to mourn him in solitude. Queen Anne wanted to be with Sarah to offer comfort, but in the depths of her grief Sarah couldn't cope with Anne's smothering presence and declined a visit, leaving the queen feeling rejected.

The couple told their friends they were finished with public life. However, they were too resilient to remain sequestered for long and eventually returned to the public sphere. Marlborough took up his military post again in Europe while Sarah returned to her position with the queen.

Since the Marlboroughs had no surviving son, the queen came up with a special act of parliament that would allow their eldest daughter, Henrietta, to inherit her father's dukedom in her own right – not her husband's – and pass it on to her son. Provisions were made in case the young man died without heirs, but such an eventuality seemed improbable.

This dynastic arrangement was a comfort to the couple, but it didn't restore Sarah's spirits. Young John Churchill's death had hit her hard. Something snapped in her and from then on she was more volatile, unpredictable and domineering than she had ever been. Marlborough returned to England and they'd had a pleasant interlude at St Albans, when suddenly she flew into a rage, accusing him of infidelity.

The duke became depressed and was plagued by migraine headaches, but he felt he had to go back to the Continent to live up to his commitments. Although Sarah went with him as far as the coast to say goodbye, their parting was devoid of their usual affection. To make matters worse, when he was boarding his ship she handed him a letter filled with accusations and grievances.

A few weeks later he received a conciliatory letter from Sarah, followed by another that was brimming with affection. Quick to forgive and forget, the duke burned the bitter document and kept the new one for the rest of his life. Sarah found it in his trunk of personal treasures after his death and realised by its condition that he must have read and re-read it many times.

As the war went on, Marlborough's resolution to go into battle with courage and daring hadn't wavered one iota. "Whatever happens to me", he wrote to Sarah before one engagement, "I beg you will believe that my heart is entirely yours."

That summer he subjected Louis XIV to his most devastating defeat. A combined French and Bavarian army had been ready to overrun Vienna, but Marlborough marched his troops through central Europe, faced the enemy near the village of Blindheim on 13 August 1704 and annihilated them. This bold, energetic commander who personally led his forces to victory was 54 years old.

At the end of the battle he wrote his most famous note to Sarah, scribbled on the back of an inn bill while he was taking a brief rest in his saddle. "I have no time to say more but to beg you will give my duty to the Queen and let her know her army has had a glorious victory. Monsieur Tallard and two other Generals are in my Coach."

It was a masterstroke of understatement. Monsieur Tallard and the "other Generals" were French commanders, now his prisoners, and the Battle of Blindheim, or as his soldiers called it, Blenheim, went down in history as the most staggering conquest by an English commander since Henry V's legendary triumph at Agincourt. Sarah took the letter to the queen, who made sure it was published in the newspapers.

Marlborough had saved Vienna and removed the threat of French dominance of Europe. The grateful Austrian emperor heaped rewards on him from gold to priceless paintings, and gave him the title of Prince of the Holy Roman Empire along with the principality of Mindelheim. His nation and his queen rewarded him and his heirs with a pension for life and a grant of the royal manor of Woodstock, where a palace would be erected and called Blenheim as a memorial to Marlborough's great achievement. To this day, Blenheim Palace is considered one of Britain's most stately edifices.

But no one thought to put a limit on the cost, and no one dreamed that the Marlborough couple would fall out of favour before construction was completed. So, for a time, it seemed that Blenheim might be on its way to becoming one of Britain's most stately white elephants.

Chapter 4
The Lustre Fades

arah and Queen Anne were growing apart. The years had shaped their characters in different ways and steered the two women in opposite directions.

The young Sarah Churchill had decided early in her career that life at court was tedious. As Duchess of Marlborough she was even more impatient with the artificial atmosphere surrounding the monarchy. Over the years, Sarah had developed a love of books and ideas, while Queen Anne was still obsessed with issues of precedence and the intricacies of royal etiquette. Anne's endless chatter about fashions, weather and gossip bored Sarah to distraction.

Further, Sarah remained true to her Whig beliefs, but Anne had begun to appreciate the notion of royal prerogative.

She was inclined to agree with the more conservative stance of the Tories, the opposition party in parliament.

Queen Anne had started making extra demands on Sarah just when she was at her busiest. Sarah had a large family needing her attention. She was overseeing the building of Marlborough House in London and quarrelling with the architect designing Blenheim. She had no time for Anne's unreasonable neediness.

The strain was showing. Sarah's quick temper was erupting too often. She deplored Anne's drift towards the Tories and preached never-ending sermons to the queen, as if she could browbeat the woman into coming to her senses.

The beginning of the end came on the day Anne inadvertently overheard Sarah refer to her as "that disagreeable person". The queen was hurt to the quick, and the love she'd felt for Sarah for more than a quarter of a century died on the spot.

Unwittingly, Sarah had set the stage for her own downfall and provided her own replacement. She'd found a position in the queen's household for her impoverished distant cousin, Abigail Masham, as a bedchamber woman.

At first, Queen Anne hadn't liked large, raw-boned Abigail, and had resented whatever time Sarah had spent with her cousin. But gradually the queen had begun to warm to the woman. Unlike Sarah, Abigail knew her place. She never argued or talked back, and she soothed away Anne's headaches with gentle fingers. And Abigail was a Tory.

Sarah was slow to realise that she was losing her hold over the queen, but once she started paying attention, it didn't take long for her to identify Abigail as her rival. Understandably, Sarah felt betrayed. But instead of taking her cue from Abigail and mending her own ways, she reacted like a scorned and jealous woman, hurling accusations and throwing tantrums.

Political events contributed to the growing tension. The Duke of Marlborough was still racking up military victories on the Continent, with the Whig majority in parliament steadfastly supporting the war effort. The Whigs decided it was time for the queen to reward them by including someone of their choice in her cabinet. The candidate they put forward was Sarah's son-in-law, Charles Spencer, the third Earl of Sunderland.

The queen flatly refused to have him. He was an extremist among the Whigs, a strident critic of the monarchy in general and of Queen Anne and her consort in particular. She detested Sunderland, just as she'd loathed his father.

Sarah pleaded her son-in-law's case. He had provoked her many times, but for the moment she was getting along with him, and Anne's rejection turned a political manoeuvre into a personal power struggle. When the queen remained unmoved, Sarah tried nagging, cajoling and bullying. But the queen would no longer be bullied.

Refusing to accept defeat, Sarah reverted to emotional and actual blackmail, threatening to publish letters Anne had written to her over the years. The potential for embarrassment was enormous. Some of Anne's written outbursts of affection for Sarah seemed more like messages to a lover than notes to a lady-in-waiting. Driving home the point, Sarah obliquely accused Anne of having a lesbian relationship with Abigail. She reduced the queen to tears and a state of nervous exhaustion – but Sarah still did not get her way.

While all these histrionics were going on, the Duke of Marlborough had won yet another victory over the French. But the English troops had suffered heavy casualties and the duke himself had barely escaped being killed. Marlborough, aware that the public at home was becoming weary of everlasting conflict, was concerned about the possibility of military cutbacks. He believed that the Grand Alliance should battle on until they were in a position to dictate peace terms to the French, and he needed an ally in the queen's cabinet to support his case. So when he returned to London, he also argued in favour of Sunderland's appointment.

The queen held out until Lord Treasurer Godolphin threatened to resign if she didn't accept Sunderland. Queen Anne valued Godolphin's services and, since he was Marlborough's close friend, feared that the latter would hand in his resignation as well. Marlborough was still a hero in the eyes of the public, and neither she nor her Tory advisers relished the thought of the controversy his departure would create. Finally the queen gave in, and Sunderland became one of her principal secretaries of state. But she never forgot that the

Marlboroughs and Godolphin had forced her hand.

Sarah clinched her downfall at a thanksgiving service at St Paul's Cathedral to celebrate the latest of her husband's victories. On the way there, she noticed that the queen wasn't wearing the jewels she had laid out for her. Deciding that Abigail had persuaded Anne to leave them off just to prove the strength of her influence, Sarah harassed the queen about the issue the whole way to St Paul's. At the cathedral, when Anne paused to say something, Sarah hissed in front of shocked onlookers, "Be quiet!"

Even Sarah knew she'd gone too far.

Later apologies from both Sarah and her husband fell on deaf ears. The queen's coldness had become impenetrable. When her consort died that autumn, Anne turned to Abigail for comfort, not to Sarah.

Sarah kept trying to regain her influence over the queen, and the tension continued building between them. Sarah repeatedly urged her husband to use his famous diplomatic skills on her behalf, and eventually he gave in and wrote to the queen.

Queen Anne's response left no doubt about her position regarding Sarah. She wrote back to the duke, saying in part, "I desire nothing but that she would leave off teasing and tormenting me, and behave herself with the decency she ought."

The End of an Era

In early 1710, the Whigs were in decline. They still agreed

with Marlborough that the war should continue until the French had been vanquished once and for all. But the Tories wanted peace, and the queen was of the same mind.

Sarah was avoiding court and staying at Windsor Lodge, making no attempts to communicate with the queen, but a new development brought her back into the fray. Queen Anne appointed a Tory to a key post in government without consulting Godolphin, her first minister. She had every right to do so, but the move was a definite snub.

Then, in June, the queen replaced Sarah's son-in-law with a Tory, even though Sarah had complained that his dismissal was an affront to the Marlborough family. Meanwhile, the peace negotiations that had begun with the allies in a strong position broke down in July. Marlborough commented on the insolence of the French delegates, saying they obviously knew he no longer had the queen's confidence. In August, Queen Anne proved him right by dismissing his good friend Godolphin and appointing a Tory to his position.

Sarah complained far and wide that Queen Anne was letting her "evil favourites" lead her by the nose. She had one more confrontation with the queen, followed by another spate of correspondence, only to run up against the wall of near-silence that Anne was so adept at erecting. Marlborough urged his wife to stay in the country and be quiet, at least until after the autumn elections, but Sarah ignored his advice.

In September, several leading Whigs resigned from

their posts to protest the conduct of the government since Godolphin's dismissal. The Tories won the October election in a landslide victory. Queen Anne, still not ready to dispense with Marlborough's services, expressed the hope that he could work with the new government.

Technically, Sarah was still in charge of the queen's private household, but in reality she wasn't welcome at court. It was inevitable that she must resign, but she wanted to do it on her own terms.

Marlborough asked his wife to write to the queen requesting permission for them to resign as a couple, at a time of their own choosing, and in a manner that would allow them a graceful exit. Queen Anne refused. She wanted to be rid of Sarah immediately while keeping Marlborough at his post.

The duke made a personal visit to the queen to ask that Sarah continue serving with him for nine more months and then make an "honourable retreat". He suggested that any other solution would reflect badly on the queen as a friend and monarch.

Unmoved, Queen Anne insisted on the return of Sarah's "Gold Key", the symbol of her power, within three days. When Marlborough relayed the order to Sarah, she handed him the key – or, according to some reports, threw it across the room – and told him to give it to the queen immediately. Sarah was 50 years old and her long career was over.

The official version of events put out at the time was that Sarah had submitted her resignation voluntarily.

Probably her possession of Anne's letters guaranteed that she was allowed that dignity.

One by one, the honours the queen had heaped on Sarah at the beginning of her reign slipped away. Queen Anne's final act of retribution against her erstwhile favourite was to cancel financial support of Blenheim Palace. Work on the opulent dwelling came to a halt.

With his wife no longer able to represent his interests at court, and with anti-war sentiment undermining the value of his status as a military hero, Marlborough was vulnerable to his political enemies. He remained in his post for another year, during which he achieved some of his greatest military triumphs.

Then the Tories accused Marlborough of corruption and threatened him with prosecution. Although the duke denied the charges, the queen unceremoniously dismissed him on 31 December 1711.

The popular press, undergoing explosive growth at this time, predictably savaged the Marlboroughs. London boasted 12 daily newspapers, many of them Tory-financed, and publishers had already discovered that stories and satires about the Duchess of Marlborough increased circulation. Her husband's humiliation was a bonanza.

"I really long as much to be out of this horrid country as I used to do to come into it," Sarah wrote after she'd had enough. Fortunately, the Tory leader had given Marlborough the option of going abroad to avoid impeachment on the corruption charges and demands for repayment of money he'd allegedly embezzled.

Faced with losing everything they'd spent their lifetime building up, the Marlboroughs chose exile. In doing so, they saved their fortune, but historians have been divided ever since on the issue of Marlborough's guilt or innocence.

They opted for Europe, where they were still treated with respect. They went to France and from there they travelled extensively. As they made their way through Germany and The Netherlands, Sarah saw Marlborough greeted as a hero. For the first time she realised just how revered he was on the Continent.

In April 1713, the Peace of Utrecht ended the long war. Sarah was appalled by the terms Britain had agreed to, and as always she expressed her opinion freely.

The Marlboroughs were in Antwerp in January 1714 when they received word that Queen Anne had fallen ill. This news probably did not upset the couple, but the next messages from England made them desperate to return home. Their daughter Elizabeth had died of smallpox, and their favourite daughter, Anne (Spencer) Sunderland, was seriously ill.

When they landed at Dover on the afternoon of 1 August, they learned that Queen Anne had died at Kensington Palace that morning. The queen's designated heir, Sophie, Electress of Hanover, had predeceased her. This left Sophie's son George – a German – next in line for the British throne.

George admired Marlborough for his military prowess. As

soon as he was crowned George I, the new monarch returned the duke to his position of military leadership, considering him the only commander capable of keeping the Jacobites at bay. Marlborough, who had considered supporting the Jacobites, decided to endorse the Hanover succession instead.

Work on Blenheim Palace resumed, but Marlborough's restoration to royal good graces had its limits. George I didn't include the duke in the inner circle of his court. The king also froze out Sunderland, though he gave the earl opportunities to prove himself in various posts.

Sunderland's wife, Anne, had recovered from the illness that had brought her parents back from Europe, but she still remained weak. Just when Sunderland had been returned to the centre of power at last, Anne developed pleurisy. The standard treatment of bloodletting caused an infection, and the Marlboroughs' beloved daughter died in the spring of 1716 at the age of 32. Shocked and distraught, Sarah raged against the incompetence of doctors, for whom she had never had much respect.

Anne had requested that her mother take care of her children, and Sarah gladly took them under her wing. The responsibility helped her cope with her sorrow.

Marlborough's grief was so terrible he suffered a stroke and fell down a staircase at Holywell House. He recovered, but only barely, and at the age of 66 was a shadow of his former self.

Years earlier, Sarah and her husband had agreed that

her fortune should be under her own control. After his debilitating stroke, she took charge of the trust administering his money as well. Using her financial power, she would try for the rest of her days – and even after her life was over – to rule her children and grandchildren with a golden fist.

The Meddling Matriarch

Sarah's widowed son-in-law, Sunderland, became First Lord of the Treasury in 1718. He remarried within 18 months of his wife's death, and when Sarah heard the news she flew into one of her towering rages. She accused him of everything she could think of, from womanising to homosexuality, ending by saying that his behaviour had killed her daughter.

Sunderland stood up to Sarah, and after their monumental battle all contact between them ended. Now wealthy in his own right, he didn't have to put up with his former mother-in-law. Not only did he have Althorp, he owned Sunderland House in Piccadilly.

But trouble was brewing. As First Lord of the Treasury, he'd been involved in encouraging citizens to exchange government bonds for shares in the South Sea Company. Along with other leading politicians, he allegedly took bribes to help keep the prices unrealistically high, allowing the early investors to make enormous gains.

Sarah bought into the scheme but sold her stock and her husband's before the South Sea bubble burst. She made a total profit of £100,000. She compounded her gains when the properties of ruined investors went up for sale and she snapped up the best of them. She selected all her purchases with typical shrewdness, but the bargain she was most pleased with was the estate of Wimbledon Park in Surrey, which had belonged to one of the directors of the South Sea Company. She bought the thousand acres of farm and woodland for £25,000 – a steal even then.

As a result of the South Sea Company scandal, Sunderland resigned from his position but was never prosecuted due to a private agreement he'd made with his successor, Sir Robert Walpole. Charles Spencer, third Earl of Sunderland, died in April 1722, leaving no one to stand as a buffer between the domineering Sarah and her Spencer grandchildren. The oldest, Robert, was now the fourth Earl of Sunderland. The second grandchild, Anne Spencer, was married to Lord Bateman, and the three youngest, Charles, John and Diana, were still at school.

Like his father and grandfather before him, Robert was addicted to gambling and had been borrowing his way into debt. He assumed Sarah would die soon and he would get her money, at least if he stayed in her good books. When a court position was offered to him, Sarah told him not to take it. She wanted nothing to do with royalty or government, and expected her grandchildren to follow her lead. Robert obeyed her command, so she rewarded him with a generous annual allowance and agreed to provide financial support for the education of his brothers, Charles and John.

Sarah moved the two younger boys from Eton to her lodgings in Windsor Great Park and hired a tutor to educate them. Then she formally adopted her favourite grandchild, Diana – or "dear little Lady Dye", as Sarah referred to her.

Diana returned her grandmother's affection and, over the ensuing years, tried her best to keep peace in a constantly warring family, but without much success.

On 12 June 1722, doctors were summoned to the bedside of a dying Duke of Marlborough. His life ended three days later. Sarah was devastated, as were the duke's surviving daughters. Sarah had been on bad terms with her daughters for several years and even the shared grief of the women did nothing to unite them. Their estrangement was so far beyond repair that at the duke's deathbed they had communicated only through third parties.

The complicated terms that had been devised by Queen Anne for the Marlborough succession passed the title to Henrietta, then to her son. If he died childless, it would then pass on to the sons of Sarah's second daughter, the late Anne Sunderland. Alternate heirs, if needed, would be the sons of Sarah's younger daughters.

In the dark days following her husband's death, Sarah took comfort in Diana. The young woman came close to marrying a Prince of Wales, just as her namesake did in the 20th century. Sarah must have suspended her aversion towards royalty when she encouraged a match between Lady Diana and Prince Frederick, heir to the throne.

An unconfirmed story claims that the wedding date had been set and the negotiations for a generous dowry from Sarah had been completed when the Tory prime minister got wind of the plans. He hastily advised the king against allowing his son to wed a granddaughter of the Duchess of Marlborough. The prince ended up marrying a German princess instead, leaving Diana to settle quite contentedly for a lesser aristocrat.

Henrietta died in 1733 after rejecting her mother's attempts at a last-minute reconciliation. By then both Henrietta's son and Anne's oldest son, Robert, had died childless, so Anne's second son, another Charles Spencer, inherited the Sunderland and the Marlborough titles. The surname of the Dukes of Marlborough would be Spencer from that time until 1817, when the family would change its name to Churchill in honour of Sarah's husband, who had been born as plain John Churchill.

Sarah's grandson had exasperated her with his excessive drinking, gambling and spending, but probably Charles's worst flaw, in Sarah's eyes, was that he looked like his father.

The hostility was mutual. Charles was receiving £8000 a year from the Marlborough trust. Feeling independent of his grandmother at last, he had boasted drunkenly that he could "kick her arse and bid her kiss his own".

Charles's profligacy dug him into a financial hole he still might have pulled himself out of if he hadn't decided to get married without consulting Sarah, choosing the daughter of a Tory peer she despised.

Sarah couldn't prevent Charles from inheriting her husband's title, but she had cut him out of her own will. And he had no claim on the Marlborough fortune except for Blenheim Palace, which would be his only after Sarah died. Even Althorp was to revert to his younger brother John, so Charles had to find another home. With his unique gift for finding ways to infuriate his grandmother, he bought a property that had belonged to Sarah's old nemesis, Abigail Masham.

Despite his transgressions, Sarah began to soften towards Charles and dropped hints about reinstating him in her will. But she refused to advance him money to pay his gambling debts, and he grew desperate. He accepted a post as colonel of a West India regiment, then moved on to a more lucrative position at court, breaking her cardinal rule against accepting royal appointments. Sarah's anger turned to blind rage when she heard that her sworn enemy Robert Walpole was behind both appointments and had said, "You see, I know the way to get everybody I have a mind to."

Sarah's attention shifted to Diana and John. Diana had been trying without success to bear a child. In 1735, she began feeling unwell and thought at first that she was pregnant again. The sad truth was that she was dying of tuberculosis, and "Lady Dye" succumbed to the wasting disease at the age of 25. True to form, Sarah lashed out in her grief, accusing Diana's husband of having killed Diana "stone dead". He was so taken aback he keeled over in a faint.

Sarah effectively now had power over only one

grandchild. John Spencer had inherited the family estate, but no title. The Sunderland earldom and the Marlborough dukedom still belonged to the errant Charles.

John – usually called Jack or Johnnie – had the same vices as his older brother but was better looking and better natured, and wasn't too proud to play by his grandmother's rules. He was sure she couldn't last much longer.

Sarah used her power as a landowner to give Johnnie the parliamentary seat of Woodstock, which was the site of Blenheim Palace, but he didn't share her interest in politics and never once spoke in the House of Commons.

In an effort to divide and conquer her remaining grand-children, Sarah offered Johnnie £40,000 if he would agree never to communicate with his brother Charles again. To his credit, Johnnie told her he loved Charles and wouldn't desert him for any amount of money. He was more ame-nable, however, to breaking ties with his sister, Lady Anne Bateman, from whom Sarah was estranged. Sarah told John she would kick him out of his quarters at Marlborough House if he didn't agree to her terms. He was living at the mansion while undergoing a long and painful treatment for a venereal disease. Rather than having to make other arrangements, he gave in.

Sarah's next demand was for Johnnie to get married and start working on her dynasty. He was willing, if not enthusiastic, and told her to go ahead and choose his bride. But Sarah wanted him to show a little more interest in the exercise. After drawing up a list of suitable candidates, she invited him to make his selection. Johnnie picked Georgina Carteret because the list was arranged in alphabetical order and her name was at the top. Almost 250 years later, a similar list would be drawn up, this one for Charles, Prince of Wales, with Diana Spencer heading it. Reportedly, the selections were determined by two of the prince's closest female confidantes – one being Camilla Parker Bowles.

The only romantic aspect of the Spencer–Carteret wedding was that it was held on St Valentine's Day in 1734. Sarah gave the couple a Palladian villa and settled £5000 a year on Johnnie and his heirs forever. Remarkably, the marriage turned out to be fairly happy and Georgina produced a male heir the following December. This son, also named John, survived in spite of fragile health that would plague him all his life. A girl followed, yet another Diana, but she died at age eight in 1743.

Sarah took her last breath on the morning of 18 October 1744. A contemporary writer remarked, "Her death in the 85th year of her life was very little regretted either by her family or the world in general."

He was probably right. Sarah must have been an extraordinarily difficult woman to deal with. But she should be credited for having created the wealth her heirs were so eager to get their hands on, and for having the stubborn grit to triumph over so many adversities during the long run of her life. Sarah was buried at Blenheim along with her duke, whose body had been waiting at Westminster Abbey since his death.

Finally, Charles, the third Duke of Marlborough, could move into Blenheim Palace – and could struggle, as his descendants have struggled ever since, to cover the enormous costs of maintaining it.

His brother Johnnie inherited the bulk of his grandmother's estate, but discovered that even from the grave Sarah had found a way to hamstring him. She'd tied up everything in trust, stipulating in her will that all the estates she had settled on Johnnie and his son would be forfeit "as if they were dead" if they ever took employment from the Crown.

Johnnie was enormously wealthy, having inherited 27 estates in 12 counties, £250,000 in assets not tied up in land, and five residences, plus paintings, priceless furnishings and the Marlborough silver. He owned Marlborough House and Sunderland House in London, as well as Althorp and Wormleighton from his father's side. But he couldn't sell anything to pay his debts or even touch the income from the property and investments, amounting to at least £30,000, so his fortune did him little good. He drank away the next 20 months of his life and then died, leaving his son John "the richest schoolboy in England".

The schoolboy would grow up without the faintest notion that money was a finite resource, even for the descendants of Sarah Marlborough. He was in for a rude awakening.

Chapter 5
The Prodigals

ohn Spencer, the sickly 11-year-old boy who inherited his great-grandmother's vast wealth, fell in love at age 16 with Georgiana Poyntz and never wavered in his devotion. Although he couldn't marry until he was 21, he refused to wait a day longer. He popped the question at his birthday party and had a minister waiting in a private room to perform the ceremony on the spot. Since Georgiana felt the same way about John, she was delighted to be swept off her feet.

The first order of business for the new couple was, as usual, to produce heirs. Since John had never been robust and was the last of his particular Spencer line, the need to fill the nursery was especially pressing.

In June 1757, Georgiana gave birth to a little girl, another

Georgiana. A boy, George John, was born prematurely in 1758 but managed to beat the odds and survive. In 1761, a second daughter, Henrietta, came along and would be known as Harriet.

Once that task had been attended to, the Spencers settled in to the standard hectic routine of aristocrats in 18th-century England. They were always on the go, entertaining and attending parties, travelling far and wide and moving from one of their five homes to another according to the time of year. They also involved themselves in the political fortunes of the Whigs.

Although the terms of Sarah's will prevented John from accepting any government or court appointments, he proved himself extremely talented at electioneering. Given his wealth, influence and aristocratic background, John needed only a title. With a little help from friends in the peerage, he was made Baron and Viscount Spencer in 1761, and four years later became the first Earl Spencer.

Lady Georgiana Spencer discovered that her husband, loving as he was, could be difficult to live with when his bad lungs were acting up, so visits to Bath and Brighton to take the waters were interspersed with longer sojourns on the Continent. Sometimes the children went along, but often they stayed home with nannies and servants for extended periods.

Georgiana was six when her parents took her as far as Spa in the Ardennes in Belgium, leaving George John and Harriet in England. When John's condition failed to improve at Spa, Lady Spencer suggested that they carry on to Italy. They parked their daughter at Antwerp with her maternal grandmother and were gone almost a year. When they returned, Georgiana was beside herself with joy. She was adorably eager to please and a model of good behaviour. She was also anxious, desperately afraid of displeasing her parents, and a compulsive worrier.

After two more siblings were born and died as babies, young Georgiana became hypersensitive to criticism and could be reduced to hysterical sobbing with one cross word. She lived in constant fear for the safety of George John and Harriet and hovered protectively over them. She was in her teens before some of the most excessive manifestations of her insecurities settled down, but even then it seems she simply learned to drive them deep within herself.

The Spencers settled into London during the "season", those months when parliament was in session. Since Marlborough House and Sunderland House had gone to the Marlborough side of the family, John decided he and his brood needed a decent city home of their own to replace their shabby Grosvenor Street residence. After finding a lot near St James's Palace, he commissioned the building of Spencer House, sparing no expense as he made the mansion a testament to his love for his wife – his very own Taj Mahal. He invested £50,000 and seven years to get Spencer House just right, then filled it with his ever-increasing collection of art, rare books and antiquities.

All that spending took quite a gouge out of the fortune Sarah Marlborough had left them, but gambling did more damage by far. John had inherited the addiction of his ancestors, and his wife was even more firmly in its grip. Spencer House became notorious for its all-night parties where the stakes were high enough to ruin a player in a single session. The Spencer children later wrote of having crept out of bed and downstairs to watch the action, and when they were older they were allowed to participate. Whatever compulsion they hadn't inherited by nature they soon acquired by nurture.

John's temper grew steadily worse as he belatedly noticed that his wealth was dwindling. He started worrying about it, yet kept right on spending and gambling. His wife threw herself into Christian charity projects, helping the poor of Althorp and setting up Sunday schools for the children, but she still found time for gambling.

Politics, however, siphoned off the largest share of the Spencer assets. In the general election in 1768, Lords Spencer, Northampton and Halifax each fielded a different candidate for the Northampton seat. "The contest of the three earls", notable for bribery – and far rougher methods of persuasion – was disastrously expensive. By the time the election was over, Halifax and Northampton were ruined and Spencer had lost an estimated £120,000, leaving him saddled with financial problems for the rest of his days.

Yet the high life of the Spencers continued and the family travelled in luxury. They were in Spa in 1773 when they met up with another regular visitor, 24-year-old William Cavendish, the fifth Duke of Devonshire. The Spencers had known William since he was a child, and for the past year speculation had been buzzing about the possibility of a match between the realm's most eligible bachelor and the elder Spencer daughter. Georgiana had grown up to be a tall, slender, graceful girl with an abundance of reddish-gold hair and expressive grey eyes, so no one was surprised when the young duke sat up and took notice of her.

Lady Spencer felt that her 16-year-old daughter was not at all ready for marriage. But the duke was a singular catch, so maternal misgivings were set aside.

The young lady herself had been spinning romantic dreams about William, and was afraid he would choose someone else before she was old enough to attract him. When she saw him in Spa and found him more attentive than usual, she allowed herself to hope she was in the running at last.

She was more than in the running. William had already made up his mind to marry Georgiana Spencer. It would be the merger of two great Whig families, two wealthy dynasties. When he felt the moment was right he proposed to her, giving every appearance of being very much in love.

Whatever "in love" meant, as the present Prince of Wales might say.

The "Hostess with the Mostest"
As a girl, Georgiana Spencer had mastered the usual social

graces of her class and time, and considerably more. She played the harp, took singing, dancing and drawing lessons, and learned etiquette and deportment. She was fluent in French and Italian, studied science and geography and practised horsemanship.

Even as a child, she'd always loved making up little plays to act out and writing verses and stories to recite to her family. As an adult she would turn out poetry and wrote a satirical novel called *The Sylph* that would go through four printings by the time she was 22. Her instinctive theatricality would also show up in her flair for the dramatic as a hostess and political leader.

Like her great-great-great-great-niece Diana Spencer, Georgiana possessed that special magic conferred on only a chosen few, a star quality that was like a magnet drawing people to her as she captivated and delighted them. By all accounts she was truly sweet, unspoiled, loving and kind. She was beloved by almost everyone who knew her – except her husband. But it seemed that even he was at least somewhat vulnerable to her charms, because although she gave him plenty of reasons over the years to demand a separation or even a divorce, he always relented and they remained together until the end of her life.

Then again, he gave her considerable cause for complaint, which she never held against him. In fact, she exhibited a self-defeating tendency to blame his transgressions on her own inadequacies. If their marriage was built on a faulty foundation and held together by extremely unconventional rules of conduct, there must have been some unbreakable bond between the Duke and Duchess of Devonshire known only to themselves.

Georgiana had wanted to marry William because she'd convinced herself she was in love with him. But she was young and far less worldly than she seemed. As a classic "pleaser", she'd confused her romantic fantasies with her intense need to win her parents' approval. And for a girl in that era and that social class, there was nothing like a proposal from the most eligible bachelor in the realm to make a lord and lady burst with pride.

Georgiana's sister, Harriet, later married William's cousin for the same reason, delighting the senior Spencers by adding a second Cavendish connection to their family tree. The Cavendish family – descendants of Bess of Hardwick – was even wealthier and more powerful than the Spencers.

The publicity surrounding the engagement of William and Georgiana was so intense that the families began to worry about hordes of curious onlookers descending on the church during the wedding. To avoid such unpleasantness, the couple said their vows in a private ceremony on 7 June 1774, two days before the planned date.

In the early days of the marriage, Georgiana brushed aside the troubling signs that the great catch she'd landed was a singularly cold fish. She told herself that William was like her father; too shy and reserved to let the world at large see what a loving softie he was inside. She believed her devotion would uncover the true William hiding behind the monosyllabic mask.

By the time she had realised that what she saw was what she would get, it was too late to change her mind. She had made her choice and lived with it.

It probably took William considerably longer to notice that he'd made a blunder. Georgiana more than lived up to his expectations as she settled into her role as chatelaine of his many estates and hostess for his social set, but her emotional needs flummoxed him. He wasn't looking for love or companionship from his wife. He wasn't interested in sitting around with her, listening to her chatter and sharing romantic dinners for two. For that sort of thing he had his club, his friends and his mistress – who had recently presented him with a daughter.

There was nothing lacking in the marriage as far as he was concerned except that his wife seemed incapable of giving him an heir. It was the one thing that mattered, and he began to resent the fact that she wasn't living up to her side of the bargain.

But he did appreciate her enthusiasm for Whig politics. His late father had been a member of the "Immortal Seven", so William had inherited the mantle of leadership whether he wanted it or not. He was more interested in the broiled blade of mutton he dined on every night at his club than in getting all fired up over the fine points of government, so when Georgiana plunged in and showed a remarkable flair for promoting the party, he was grateful.

The new Duchess of Devonshire began her involvement in politics at the Public Days that were a family tradition at the Chatsworth estate in Derbyshire. Public Days were a long tradition dating back to feudal times but had turned into the equivalent of local political rallies. Once a week the duke and duchess dressed up in their finery to greet any and all comers to an open house featuring groaning buffet tables and plenty of ale and wine. Before long, Georgiana had proven herself a natural at making every person there feel like her own special guest.

At balls held in the district towns she would dance the nights away in stifling heat and the crush of too many bodies – some of them falling-down-drunk – and keep smiling, learning people's names and showing interest in their problems. A natural political animal in a time when women couldn't vote or hold office, she gradually chipped away at the male edifice of power until she'd carved out her own special niche.

When in London, she organised supper parties and other entertainments at Devonshire House that quickly became the most coveted invitations among the *Ton*, the elite few – at most 1200 people – who were wealthy and influential enough to be arbiters of fashion, manners and morality. Even jaded cynics remarked on her infectious charm and appealing lack of artifice.

"The Duchess of Devonshire is the most envied woman

of the day in the *Ton*", a newspaper reported within a year of her marriage. Publishers had discovered that having a story about the delightful duchess in their publications would increase sales – just as they did more than 200 years later when Princess Diana made her debut on the world stage.

In Georgiana's time, as in Sarah Marlborough's, the British press was at a point of explosive growth and was highly competitive. Georgiana quickly caught on that she could use the popularity of newspapers and periodicals for her own purposes. She proved to be as brilliant at the game as Diana did when it was her turn.

The Duchess of Devonshire could start a fashion just by trying something out herself, however ridiculous it might be. She took the trend for high hairdos to its ludicrous extreme, using padding and pomade to create three-foot towers decorated with such whimsies as stuffed birds, waxed fruit, miniature tableaux and a ship in full sail. Other women adopted the style even though the elaborate construction took hours to create and turned the ladies into walking fire hazards in that world of blazing chandeliers. They were even willing to suffer the indignity of sitting on the floor of their coaches whenever they went anywhere.

Georgiana led the craze for the Turkish fashion in clothing, then introduced the little muslin chemise tied at the middle with a simple ribbon. The Queen of France, Marie Antoinette, had sent it to her. The French queen had created a scandal by posing for a portrait in the simple white dress that looked like a nightgown, but as soon as Georgiana showed up in her silver-sprigged muslin at the Prince of Wales's ball, every lady in town had to have one. Ultimately it became the signature look for the Regency and Napoleonic periods in Britain and France.

Georgiana's flair for fashion included design. She created the buff-and-blue uniform that at first signified Whig support for the struggles of the American Colonies against the rigid authoritarianism of King George III. The uniform, worn by many Whig supporters, eventually became identified with the whole Whig philosophy. But Georgiana did more than influence the political party's dress code. More importantly, she organised other aristocratic women into teams of on-the-street canvassers during elections.

It seemed that almost anything Georgiana did became useful to the Whigs. She adopted the peculiar drawl of her Cavendish in-laws, an odd mix of baby talk and unorthodox pronunciation. The word "you" became "oo", her name was said as "George-ayna", the colour "yellow" was "yaller". If the Duchess of Devonshire spoke that way, so did everyone in her set, and the Devonshire drawl was identified so closely with her political affiliation, it became one of the key signs of Whiggism by the middle of the next century.

Because Georgiana was such a recognisable icon, merchants and manufacturers cashed in on her popularity. The top purveyor of perfumes and toiletries to the gentry in London found out which French hair powder was Georgiana's favourite, bought it up and marketed it as Devonshire Powder. Josiah Wedgwood named his Devonshire china pattern in her honour. Georgiana herself came up with a colour known as "Devonshire brown".

A minor scandal once erupted when one of Georgiana's seamstresses took bribes from other aristocratic ladies to slip them a drawing of her latest creation. Each woman thought she was stealing an original until they all showed up at a ball in identical gowns.

One of Georgiana's flashier ideas came shortly after the Montgolfier brothers amazed the court of Versailles in 1783 with the launch of a hot-air balloon over the royal palace. When two of their imitators were in Britain in 1784, Georgiana held dinners at Devonshire House in their honour. One of them, an Italian, wore a Devonshire brown silk coat in her honour when he was invited to court, and she talked the other, a Frenchman named Blanchard, into making his last ascent in Britain a Whig occasion. She persuaded the Prince of Wales and 100 Whigs and their ladies to show up at Grosvenor Square on a chilly December day in their blue and buff uniforms to watch her release the ropes – decorated with blue-and-buff ribbons, of course – in front of huge crowds of onlookers. From then on Blanchard's balloon was called the "Devonshire Aerial Yacht". Georgiana instinctively understood the power of symbolism to implant an idea.

As uncontested leader of the Devonshire Circle, that select mix of artists, writers, actors, politicians and aristocrats who congregated at Devonshire House, Georgiana patronised the arts and helped establish the careers of some of the most celebrated stars of the theatre and concert stage.

Through Georgiana's efforts, Whigs began to be linked in the public mind with wit and elegance. This positive image was the bane of the ruling party, who worried about Whig gains. "She really is a very good politician," one rival conceded. "As soon as ever any young man comes from abroad he is immediately invited to Devonshire House and to Chatsworth – and by that means he is to be of the Opposition."

But there was a price to be paid for all that popularity, and it would be steep.

Days of Wine and Roses – and Thorns

The downside of celebrity, as Georgiana discovered, was that an icon could also be a target. The same newspapers that glorified the glamorous duchess also made fun of her, often cruelly. When her political opponents perceived her as a serious threat, they poured money into the coffers of any publisher willing to sully her reputation.

Sometimes she made it all too easy. She wasn't the only woman who went out canvassing in neighbourhoods where a lady of her station was an unusual sight, but not many others would be found in a pub chatting up the locals over a pint of ale. Georgiana was blistering her feet on the cobblestone streets on behalf of her candidate, Charles Fox, helping to present him as the "Man of the People". But by association she became the "Woman of the People", which in those days had an entirely different and extremely negative connotation.

The unregulated newspapers took the concept of a free press to new depths as they accused Georgiana of trading kisses and even sexual favours for votes. While she was winning the hearts of the people by talking to voters as equals, listening to their problems and hearing about the issues they considered important, her enemies were printing lewd cartoons to be pasted on walls and fences and distributed to men's clubs and barbershops.

When she found it all too much to endure, she retreated to Holywell House in St Albans to hide out with her mother, only to be urged back into the fray by her Cavendish in-laws, who otherwise had little use for her. But at least they promised to fight on her behalf, and the fact that they kept that promise indicates how important she was to their cause. Battalions of workers ripped down anti-Georgiana posters almost as soon as they were pasted up, and newspapers faced lawsuits and other forms of retribution if they libelled her.

Despite her experience with the press, Georgiana remained naïve in many respects. Even friends took advantage of her trusting nature. A member of the Devonshire Circle, the playwright Richard Sheridan, used her as a model for a character named Lady Teazle in his Drury Lane play, *School for Scandal*. Although Georgiana was, as always, a good sport about the unflattering caricature and went with the rest of her crowd to support the play's opening night, she was a little taken aback. "I am afraid that the minute I think seriously of my conduct", she told her mother in a letter, "I shall be so shocked."

It never seemed to occur to her that she should have been shocked instead at Sheridan for abusing her friendship.

What made Georgiana especially vulnerable to attacks in the press was that she was harbouring a secret. Addicted to gambling, she had started piling up debts early in her marriage. The alarm bells started going off when her losses added up to more than her generous annual allowance. Georgiana heard the din but tried to drown it out with the happier noise of revelry. She stayed at the gaming tables long after she should have walked away.

She was afraid to tell her husband about her debts, so they kept mounting. Even when she finally worked up the courage to confess – or had no other option – she couldn't bring herself to reveal their full extent. Inevitably her private troubles made it into the public eye, which brought her to the brink of marital disaster. Her husband started talking about a separation.

Yet he was no angel himself, and Georgiana's generous nature had made things easier for him than he had any right to expect. When his mistress died, Georgiana not only accepted his illegitimate daughter into their home, she welcomed her with open arms, thrilled to have a child to love.

William began a very public affair with Georgiana's friend Lady Jersey, for whom part of the sexual excitement was making sure Georgiana and everyone else in society knew about it. Georgiana didn't kick up a fuss. Her parents finally stepped in and told the illicit pair to break it off or pay the social consequences, but all Georgiana ever said was that she'd begun to feel a little uneasy around Lady Jersey.

Instead of punishing others, Georgiana punished herself. Her gambling intensified and her losses piled up. The debts gave her sleepless nights so she turned to opiates. Periodically she threw herself into an effort to reform, reporting to her ever-vigilant mother about her good works, her church attendance and her immersion in prayer. She developed eating disorders, sometimes closeting herself in her room for a week of self-denial that ended in a return to all-night drinking sessions and eating binges. Her weight fluctuated and she suffered frequent miscarriages. Hating herself for that failure, she let herself be pulled back into the maelstrom of her personal vicious circle.

If Georgiana had been as kind to herself as she was to others, she might have considered the possibility that her emotional roller-coaster, as well as her inability to produce a child, could have been the duke's fault as much as hers. It seemed his approach to conception was to barge into Georgiana's room after an all-night session at his club and do what had to be done. To William, of course, the blame was entirely hers. Then they met Bess.

Georgiana and William were on one of their visits to Bath to take the waters when Georgiana's mother asked her to get in touch with Lady Elizabeth Foster while she was there. Lady Elizabeth, the daughter of one of Lady Spencer's friends, was separated from her husband and had lost custody of her children. She was living in Bath with her aunt and subsisting on a pittance.

Georgiana dutifully made contact with Lady Elizabeth, who turned out to be an extremely pretty, vibrant young lady with dark hair framing an oval face – not at all the pitiful creature Georgiana had expected to find. In no time Lady Elizabeth, nicknamed Bess, had become Georgiana's dearest friend, and even William seemed to like her. He agreed to invite Bess to accompany them to nearby Plympton, where he was attending summer camp with the volunteer militia.

As the threesome spent the summer together, Bess brought about an amazing transformation in the Devonshire marriage. Witty and effervescent, she made both Georgiana and William laugh. She flirted with the duke and offered warmth and understanding to the duchess, livening up their evenings by reading aloud passages from her favourite risqué novels. Before they left Plympton, Georgiana was at long last pregnant.

From that time on, Bess was an integral part of their lives. She was Georgiana's confidante and eventually became the duke's mistress. Except for long periods when Bess travelled in Europe on her own, the three of them were a close-knit family. If there were times when Bess's resentment of her secondary role made her try to gain the upper hand, the sheer purity of Georgiana's affection shamed her into returning the feelings in full measure.

Lady Spencer didn't like Bess or the unconventional arrangement in her daughter's household, and she particularly resented the gossip it aroused. Speculation about the nature of the odd relationship kept the *Ton* amused and the newspapers busy with innuendo. Even today, controversy surrounds their *ménage à trois*. No one can say for certain what went on behind closed doors, since letters that might have shed some light on the subject have been heavily censored by succeeding generations.

Bess did become pregnant by the duke, not once but twice. She went off to Italy to have the first child in secret, not even telling Georgiana until much later. But when the second baby was on the way, Bess informed her friend immediately. Georgiana's reaction was to offer to go to France with Bess to take care of her while she had the baby, but her disapproving mother talked her out of that plan.

Georgiana's marriage, however, was in trouble. In 1789, after they had been together for 15 years, Georgiana and William were close to breaking up. William had reached the end of his tether with Georgiana's compulsive gambling, her astronomical debts and, most of all, her failure to give him a male heir. By that time, she'd given birth to two girls and he was losing hope. Bess, by contrast, had given him a girl and a boy. And Bess was the one he wanted.

Georgiana was in a panic. Aware that her only claim

on her husband was that she was still his wife and therefore the only one who could give him a legitimate heir, she was desperate to have another child. Reasoning that if she could escape the constant tension of being hounded by her creditors she might relax enough to get pregnant, produce a son and earn the duke's forgiveness, she somehow talked him into taking the whole family to France for an extended holiday – Bess included.

They left Dover and crossed the Channel in June. Even Lady Spencer joined them for the trip, setting aside her extreme dislike of Bess. The vacation landed them right in the middle of the opening salvos of the French Revolution, but that small detail didn't stop the intrepid travellers. They were visiting Georgiana's friend Marie Antoinette in Versailles at the very moment when the French people who had marched from Paris forced their way in to see the king.

Oddly, none of these aristocrats, English or French, seemed to grasp the full significance of what was happening. Even the howling mobs didn't trouble them except as a passing nuisance.

The party went to Spa, where Georgiana finally got her miracle. She became pregnant. All she had to hope for was that she would carry the baby to term and give birth to a boy. She still didn't want to go back to London and face her creditors, so the group carried on to Brussels, minus the duke. William had to go home to take care of a crisis in the marriage of Georgiana's sister, Harriet, and her difficult husband, his cousin.

As Georgiana's due date drew closer, Brussels turned dangerous. Signs of imminent revolution were flaring up even there. Inexplicably, the travellers decided to head back to Paris and had almost reached their goal when Georgiana went into labour. Lady Spencer took charge. First, she sent Bess ahead with instructions to go to the opera and be seen. She wanted to make certain that no one could say later that the child was Bess's rather than Georgiana's, a rumour she'd already been made aware of through letters from friends. She contacted an acquaintance whose home in Passy was available and made the necessary arrangements for Georgiana to have her child there. To everyone's immense relief, when the baby arrived it was a boy.

In August the family went home, but the birth of William George Spencer Cavendish hadn't ended Georgiana's troubles after all. Her husband still didn't want to pay her huge debts. So Georgiana did what Georgiana would always do when she was in trouble. She found more trouble.

All for one and one for all
Charles Grey was an up-and-coming Whig politician who'd been flirting with Georgiana for years. He finally managed to seduce her after her son was born. She was infatuated, mesmerised and indiscreet. In the spring of 1791, Georgiana discovered she was going to have another child, this one Grey's.

Bess and Harriet knew about the pregnancy from the

outset and tried to help Georgiana keep it secret. They were all staying in Bath, but a doctor told Harriet she should seek a warm climate for the sake of her health. The possibility of going away with her sister seemed to be Georgiana's only hope of having the baby without her husband's knowledge, but she had to get his permission and she wasn't sure how to go about it.

Still in Bath, she was in her sixth month and showing her pregnancy very obviously when William unexpectedly arrived. Someone in London had told him he should see his wife immediately.

When he confronted Georgiana she didn't try to pretend the child was his, and he was beside himself with outrage. Harriet was in the next room becoming increasingly nervous as she heard shouting and crying from behind the closed doors. Then the duke summoned Bess and berated her for covering up for Georgiana.

He ordered Georgiana to go abroad immediately to have the baby, leaving her other children behind. He gave her a choice. She could renounce Charles Grey, give up the baby for adoption and stay away until she was given permission to return home, or she could face a divorce and never see her legitimate children again.

For Georgiana it wasn't a choice at all. She was deeply in love with Grey and dreaded giving up his child, but to be separated permanently from her two daughters and her little son was not an option. When she told Charles Grey her decision, he couldn't forgive her. Writing to a friend, Georgiana said that he was "very cruel" but, true to form, she didn't blame him and insisted that he was "deserving of pity too".

Harriet took it for granted that she would go into exile with her sister but was surprised when her husband, who had a soft spot for Georgiana, said he would tag along with them and help in any way he could. Then Bess announced that she too would share Georgiana's banishment.

Even Lady Spencer joined the ever-expanding entourage. Georgiana's brother, George John, lent his quiet support by paying for the services of a doctor and a business agent to accompany the travellers and help them along the way. This kind of backup was invaluable, since Georgiana possessed nothing but the contents of her baggage, and William had forbidden her to borrow from anyone.

Alone in London with his righteous anger, the duke started drinking heavily and talking about legal separation, listening to the malevolent urgings of his relatives. He left his children in the care of a nurse and didn't see them throughout his wife's long exile. His baby son kept saying over and over, "Mama gone, Mama gone."

Charles Grey's daughter was born in Montpelier in the south of France. Georgiana handed her over to a foster mother to be nursed. When the baby was old enough to travel she would be taken to Grey's parents in Northumberland to be brought up as his sister.

With her part of the bargain fulfilled, Georgiana hoped

the banishment would end. The others were also restless to return home, but the duke hadn't finished punishing his wife. He wrote that Bess could do what she liked but Georgiana was to stay away.

What Bess liked was travel, so she played tour guide as the merry little band made its way through Nice, Switzerland and Italy. There were nervous moments along the way, with threats of attacks from brigands and revolutionaries always within the realm of possibility, but apart from Georgiana's intense longing for her children, the exiles were having a thoroughly pleasant time.

Georgiana rediscovered the intellectual pursuits of her childhood. She studied music, science, drawing and languages, and took up chemistry and mineralogy. She filled her letters to the children with sketches and maps, descriptions and lively histories. A poem she wrote and dedicated to them, *Passage of the Mountain of St Gothard*, earned enough kudos to be published some years later in French, Italian and German, and is still the subject of literary interest today.

William didn't relent until the revolution took a threatening turn in 1793 with the execution of Louis XVI. Georgiana was shattered by the news from Paris and anxious about Marie Antoinette, but she was grateful to be able to go home at last. Harriet's health had taken a turn for the worse so she and Lady Spencer stayed in Italy. Both sisters were upset when they had to separate.

The duke met Georgiana and Bess in a smart new

carriage when they arrived in England and drove them back to Devonshire House, where the servants lined up to welcome them home with a display of warmth, affection and relief. But Georgiana found that her children had suffered from her long absence even more than she'd feared. It took all her patience to try to rebuild her relationship with them.

She kept her word not to see Charles Grey and never acknowledged his daughter as hers, though she eventually obtained permission to visit the little girl from time to time in the role of an indulgent godmother.

Grey caused his former lover a great deal of pain when he married in 1795 without sending her a hint of advance warning. In true Georgiana style, she coped with her sorrow by befriending his wife.

For the next while Georgiana poured her energy into writing essays, poetry and even a song for one of Richard Sheridan's plays. She continued with her chemistry studies, attended science lectures and became knowledgeable enough as a mineralogist to leave a museum-quality collection to Chatsworth. She even converted a room at Devonshire House into a laboratory where she conducted her own experiments.

But after all she'd been through and all the vows she'd made to herself, she couldn't stop gambling.

In 1796, Georgiana began suffering chronic eye infections. Doctors tried everything from strangling her in the hope of increasing the flow of blood to the eye – and nearly killing her in the process – to applying leeches directly to the eyeball. She underwent an operation without anaesthetic, which she reportedly "bore with great courage", but lost the eye. With her looks ravaged she hated appearing in public, though she managed to show up at gaming tables.

Bess, meanwhile, remained based with Georgiana and William but travelled extensively on the Continent and tried to find a husband of her own instead of sharing the duke.

The political influence of the Devonshire Circle ebbed as war with France and fear of the revolutionary principles taking hold across the Channel made Whig policies fall into disfavour.

In 1804, Georgiana's older daughter, by this time herself a mother of two children, vindicated Georgiana when she wrote: "One cannot know till one has separated from you how different you are from everyone else, how superior to all mothers, even good ones."

Georgiana enjoyed one last hurrah as the darling of the Whigs when they were returned to government. She played an important behind-the-scenes role in the formation of a new cabinet consisting of the most important men in her life, including her brother, George John, and friends Charles Fox, Charles Grey and Richard Sheridan.

She gave her last Devonshire House supper party wearing spectacles with black crêpe over the lens to shield her from light, but still suffered blinding headaches afterwards.

That year, she caught a chill and took to her bed, but

when she didn't bounce back her doctors discovered that she had a liver abscess. They did their worst, putting her through days of unnecessary, useless torment.

Georgiana died on 30 March 1806 at the age of 49. Harriet never fully recovered from the loss and Bess wrote in her journal, "Saturday was a day of horror beyond all words to express ... how can I live without her who was the life of my existence!"

England's most beloved duchess lay in state for five days while a steady line of mourners paid their respects. Huge crowds gathered outside Devonshire House to share their grief. The Prince of Wales – often alleged to be one of Georgiana's lovers, though more likely one of her close platonic friends – summed up the general feelings when he said, "The best-natured and best-bred woman in England is gone."

Three years later, Bess and the duke were married. As soon as she was his wife he went out and found himself a new mistress, but survived just two more years. Unable to achieve Georgiana's success in London society, Bess moved to Rome and became involved with a cardinal of the Roman Catholic Church.

The Spencer dynasty was relatively quiet for the next few generations, producing royal equerries and ladies-in-waiting, a bona fide saint and a Viceroy of Ireland.

Then along came a high-spirited Yankee gal to help spice up the genetic stew.

Chapter 6
The Rebels

Diana's great-grandfather, James Boothby Roche, was a wickedly good-looking fortune hunter with an extra shot or two of blarney in his blood. His father, the second Baron Fermoy, had lost his estates in Ireland due to political disorder. After the baron's death, Jim's brother had inherited the title and whatever was left of the family's wealth, which he proceeded to gamble away.

Not content to live in poverty, Jim followed a rainbow to America to look for the pot of gold he was sure was waiting there for him. But by the time he'd tried prospecting for gold in the Yukon, cattle ranching in Wyoming and other get-rich-quick schemes, he'd decided there had to be an easier way.

He returned to England in the late 1870s as broke as

ever. But he was still a member of an aristocratic family and a handsome bachelor, so London's leading hostesses showered him with invitations. An extra male was always welcome at a dinner party.

Jim attended a gathering at the home of Jennie Churchill, the American-born mother of Britain's future prime minister, Sir Winston Churchill. Jennie introduced Jim to pretty, auburn-haired Fanny Work, her childhood friend from New York. When Jim gazed into Fanny's big brown eyes, he saw opportunity shining back at him, while Fanny saw romance and the man of her dreams. All Jim had to do was turn on a bit of his roguish charm and she was his. By the time she was boarding a ship to sail back to New York, she had accepted Jim's proposal.

But she had to figure out how to tell her father about the engagement. Franklin Work, a self-made millionaire and ultra-patriot, was infuriated by the recent trend that saw impoverished European bluebloods solving their financial problems by latching onto Yankee heiresses. "International marriages should be a hanging offence!" he'd thundered, and decreed that his daughters would wed good solid American men or lose their inheritance.

People who knew Jim Roche warned 22-year-old Fanny that he wasn't husband material, but she returned to England in 1880 and married him anyway. Franklin made good on his threat and disinherited her, but he had settled a considerable sum of money on her already, so she and Jim had no financial problems when they set up their household in London.

But Jim turned out to be a gambler, a philanderer and a spendthrift. By the time he and Fanny had produced twin sons and a daughter in quick succession, she was thoroughly disillusioned. They were out of money and Jim was treating her "abominably". After 11 years of trying to hold things together, she collected her children and went home to New York, putting her pride in her otherwise empty pocket.

Franklin undoubtedly enjoyed his I-told-you-so moment but reinstated Fanny and added all three of her children to his will – on condition that she would divorce her husband, drop her married name and title, and never return to Europe.

Fanny swallowed whatever objections she might have had to her father's terms and divorced her husband in 1891. During the proceedings, Jim's efforts to win a generous settlement for himself infuriated Franklin, who added a codicil to his will stating that his grandchildren would inherit their portion of his legacy only if they never set foot in Great Britain.

In 1903, Fanny fell in love again, this time with a Hungarian named Cohen who ran her father's stables and called himself Auriel Batonyi. When she ran off to marry him, Franklin, true to form, disinherited her once more. Three years later, with another divorce under her belt, she was back in Daddy's good graces and his will.

Franklin had been taking care of Fanny's children, giving the boys an expensive Harvard education. When he died in 1911 at age 92, he left them each a fortune. To receive it, however, they would have to become American citizens and agree to stay in the United States for the rest of their lives.

The twins, Maurice and Frank, didn't care for such draconian restrictions. They mulled over the problem until they realised that the solution was staring them in the face. All they had to do was contest the terms of the will. Since none of the other beneficiaries offered objections, they won their case. Fanny gleefully took her share and sailed off to Paris to spend the rest of her days as part of the international fast set until she passed away in 1947 at the age of 89. Her will provided legacies for her grandchildren and even great-grandchildren, yet unborn. Diana Spencer and her siblings each received £60,000 when they turned 18 in the 1970s.

The twins' father, Jim Roche, had inherited his brother's title, so when he died in 1920 it went to Maurice, the twin who had emerged first from the womb. Frank, shy and timid, probably wouldn't have wanted it anyway, whereas tall, handsome Maurice was to the manor born. Gregarious and easy-going, Maurice exuded confidence and enjoyed being a baron even though the title came with no material estate. He headed for England to take up his aristocratic heritage.

Still single at the age of 36, Maurice was a popular bachelor but didn't marry until 10 years later. His bride was Ruth Gill, the bright, attractive daughter of a middle-class Aberdeen landowner. A talented pianist, Ruth was on the brink of a career on the concert stage, but Chopin and Beethoven didn't stand a chance against the dashing Baron Fermoy.

Besides his good looks, *bon vivant* manner and independent wealth, Maurice had top-drawer social connections. He had become a close personal friend of the Duke of York, King George V's second son. As a favour to his son, the king granted the lease for Park House on the royal Sandringham estate to Baron Fermoy. Ruth liked the idea of having a royal duke and duchess as neighbours. When Maurice proposed to her, she didn't give the 26-year age difference between them a moment's thought. She became his baroness and moved into Park House, where she developed a close friendship with Elizabeth, Duchess of York.

In 1934, Ruth gave birth to a daughter, Mary Cynthia. Two years later a second girl came along, Frances Ruth. Frances was born on 20 January 1936, the day King George V died at Sandringham. The king's older son, David, succeeded to the throne as Edward VIII. Within a year, the new king gave up his throne to marry an American divorcée, scandalising his country, forcing his younger brother to become George VI and earning the lifelong enmity of his sister-in-law, the new Queen Elizabeth.

Duty before all was Elizabeth's motto, and her friend Ruth, Baroness Fermoy, agreed. In time it became abundantly clear that, for Ruth, duty to Their Royal Majesties took precedence over all other considerations, even the well-being of her own family.

Frances and Johnnie

On 1 June 1954, Ruth's younger daughter, Frances Roche, married Johnnie Spencer, heir to the Spencer earldom, at Westminster Abbey. The press described the event as the wedding of the year. Queen Elizabeth II led the contingent of royal guests including Prince Philip, the Queen Mother and Princess Margaret, along with six other members of the realm's first family.

The 18-year-old bride wore silk faille encrusted with crystals and studded with small floral sprays of diamonds. Her veil was attached to the Spencer diamond tiara. As she walked towards her groom on the arm of her still-handsome father, Frances was nervous and trembling.

Johnnie Spencer, Viscount Althorp, was waiting for his bride at the end of the long aisle, silently encouraging her with a smile. He must have been relieved to see her. Snarled traffic had made the queen's car four minutes late, and a message had been sent to Frances and her father to slow down their own progress to the Abbey. The groom, having no idea what had happened, had been left to wonder whether he'd been abandoned at the altar.

After the ceremony and the signing of the register by the royal witnesses, the couple emerged from the Abbey, arms linked as they walked under the raised swords of an honour guard from Johnnie's regiment. Frances was now Viscountess Althorp and knew her primary duty was to produce a male heir. By the time she and Johnnie returned from their two-month honeymoon, she was happily expecting a baby.

But Frances didn't get it quite right the first time. She gave birth to a girl, Elizabeth Sarah Lavinia Spencer, who would be called Sarah. Frances was thrilled with her daughter and Johnnie was pleased as well, though they both understood from his father's forced smile that they'd better start trying again, and soon.

That summer, Frances's father died of cancer. He'd been an MP for King's Lynn for 13 years, a true champion of the people, admired and trusted by his constituents. He had the gift of making people feel important, genuinely caring about them, always ready to help them solve their problems. "My father had no interest in whether you lived in a castle, a croft or a caravan," Frances later said of him. "He was only interested in the person."

Just after her 21st birthday in 1957, Frances bore a second daughter, Cynthia Jane, known as Jane. Around that time, the Queen Mother offered Ruth a place at court, making her one of her Women of the Bedchamber. Since Ruth would no longer be living at Park House, she suggested that Frances and Johnnie take over the lease. The young family moved into the home where Frances had grown up.

Frances was delighted, and for Johnnie the chance to move out of the cottage he and Frances had been occupying on the Althorp estate represented freedom. He couldn't wait to put some distance between himself and his harsh, incessantly critical father.

Once Johnnie and Frances had taken over Park House, he rarely visited Althorp or saw his father, though he remained close to his mother, Cynthia, Countess Spencer. The former Cynthia Hamilton was a beautiful, sweet-natured woman. Judging by her portrait, Diana's resemblance to her was striking.

Before her marriage, Cynthia had been touted as a possible bride for the Prince of Wales, but she had accepted Jack Spencer's proposal and the prince had gone on to marry the American divorcée who would cost him his throne.

Jack was an irascible husband and an austere father, more interested in Althorp and its contents than in his family, and over the years Cynthia had acquired the role of peacemaker. She was described by one visitor to Althorp as being "like a goddess, distilling charm and gentleness around her". Her children and grandchildren adored her. She was the one who dispensed hugs and organised Easter egg hunts.

Despite being in his early 30s and having a wife and two daughters, Johnnie still wasn't sure what he wanted to do with his life while he waited to inherit Althorp. He thought farming might be a good idea, but he had no land of his own and no money to purchase it. Frances took £20,000 of the inheritance she'd received from her late grandmother, Fanny Work, and invested it in 600 acres for Johnnie to cultivate.

For a while, Johnnie was happy. He even got along well with his mother-in-law, who was only 16 years his senior. Frances was pleased that her husband liked Ruth, until it dawned on her that the two of them had started joining forces and frequently took each other's side against her. As the years went by and Frances failed to provide a Spencer son, she couldn't shake the feeling that her mother blamed her for letting the family down.

In early 1960, Frances finally gave birth to a boy. He would be called John, the traditional name of a firstborn Spencer male. The baby was born in the master bedroom at Park House, with the aid of a midwife. Moments after his birth, the room was abuzz with whispers and frenzied activity. No one explained to the groggy new mother what was going on, and she was beginning to panic when Johnnie arrived to stay by her side. The infant was whisked off to the nursery.

Then Johnnie was called away, and Frances was left alone. She could hear hushed voices from outside the room, first her husband's, then her mother's. Frances remained isolated for hours, all the while knowing something was horribly wrong.

At last someone came back to tell her that her baby was dead and that his body had already been taken away. She'd had no chance to see or hold him, a loss that haunted her for the rest of her life. Johnnie and Ruth decided that Frances should be told that the child had been born with unformed lungs. For whatever reason, they withheld the truth, that he had suffered extensive malformation.

As soon as Frances was back on her feet, Johnnie and

Ruth decided she should undergo a round of medical tests to find out why she couldn't seem to bear a healthy male. Unaware that a father's genes determine the sex of his off-spring, most people at that time blamed some unknown inadequacy in the mother. By the time Frances had been through a battery of unpleasant and humiliating tests, she'd slid into a dark depression. Yet the efforts to conceive continued.

When she discovered she was pregnant again, Frances decided to keep her condition to herself as long as possible. She took Sarah and Jane to the seaside in Devon for a brief holiday, just the three of them. While there she suffered another miscarriage, alone in the bathroom, sobbing. Frances didn't tell anyone what had happened until years later, when she confided in her grown children about the loss.

By the autumn of that same year she was expecting again. She chose to keep quiet about this pregnancy, too; at least until she was reasonably sure she would carry the baby to term. By the time her due date rolled around she was terrified she might have trouble because of the miscarriage, but on 1 July 1961 another little girl came into the world with relative ease. The parents christened the baby Diana Frances at a church in Sandringham. A healthy, beautiful child, Diana was all big blue eyes and soft skin. Frances adored her.

But she knew she had failed again. Perhaps the extent of her family's frustration was revealed by the fact that Diana was the first of the Spencer children not to have a member of the royal family as a godparent.

Frances understood her husband's desire for a son. The urgency arose from the rules of primogeniture, a deeply entrenched system dating back centuries. If Johnnie died without a male heir, the Spencer earldom and the estates and assets that went with it would go to his cousin Bobby Spencer. Frances and her daughters wouldn't even be able to stay at Althorp, and their inheritance would consist only of whatever savings Johnnie had accumulated personally in his lifetime. He treasured his daughters, but he needed a son.

Three years later, Frances was pregnant again. She was booked into a room at a London clinic and in May 1964 was delivered of a healthy boy. He was christened Charles Edward Maurice in Westminster Abbey, with the Queen herself as his godmother. Flags flew over Althorp to celebrate his birth.

By this time Frances was in her late 20s. She was beginning to want more out of life than doddering around in the country with an increasingly boring husband. As a youngster she had been a headstrong daredevil, happiest when she was dancing barefoot on the rooftop between the chimneystacks to the rhythm of the tune playing in her imagination. Careful schooling and Ruth's strict discipline had suppressed her natural ebullience, and the constant pregnancies in the early years of her marriage had kept her subdued. But now the real Frances was struggling to reappear.

She had done her bit for the dynasty, and her marriage was dead. There was nothing left to do but bury it.

"The Bolter"

The Spencer marriage had started with the wedding of the year and it ended in the scandal of the year when Frances left Johnnie for Peter Shand Kydd. In hindsight, the unfolding of events was inevitable. Once Johnnie had fathered his heir, he seemed to lose interest in his wife, and she began spending more and more time in London.

When she was at Althorp both she and Johnnie drank heavily, and the constant tension flared up into ferocious quarrels, which were loud and sometimes violent. "It was a very unhappy childhood," Diana confessed much later. "Parents were busy sorting themselves out. I remember seeing my father slap my mother across the face and I was crying on the floor ... Mummy was crying an awful lot."

But in 1967, the fights suddenly ended. Frances was in London more often, supposedly shopping. She'd taken a small flat in the city and Johnnie was satisfied that all she'd needed was time to get over all those pregnancies. Even when she was home at Park House she seemed more contented, and the heavy drinking stopped. With Sarah and Jane at boarding school in West Heath, Frances had more time to spend with the younger children. But it was the calm before the storm. Frances had fallen in love.

She and Johnnie had been friends with Peter and Janet Shand Kydd for some time, and in late February of that year had gone on a 10-day skiing holiday with them to Switzerland. It turned out to be 10 days that shook their world. Always drawn to each other, Frances and Peter realised in Switzerland that their friendship had turned into something deeper.

Johnnie found out about the affair in September, right after the older girls had gone back to boarding school. Johnnie confronted Frances and they went at each other in a final set-to. Shouting how tired she was of the marriage, Frances packed her bags and stormed out of the house.

Diana and Charlie were in the nursery and crept downstairs, where they saw the front door standing slightly ajar. They peeked out and saw their father angrily hefting their mother's suitcases into the boot of her car while the verbal battle went on and on. Then Frances got behind the wheel and screeched away. Johnnie strode back into the house and slammed into his study, passing the children without a word.

Charlie, who was only three, started weeping quietly, clinging to his six-year-old sister. No one explained anything to them. All they knew was that their mother was gone and they were afraid they would never see her again.

At night in his room, Charlie cried for his mother while Diana, afraid of the dark, tried and failed to summon the courage to go to him. She was paralysed by her phobia and tormented by guilt for failing Charlie. As children will, she decided she must have done something terrible for such an awful thing to happen to her family.

But eventually Charlie and Diana did see their mother

again. They joined her in London, where she'd enrolled Diana at a school near her flat and planned special outings and treats for both youngsters. They settled into a pleasant routine and Charlie stopped crying at night. They visited their father on weekends, but he'd never been as involved a parent as Frances and wasn't comfortable with his children.

Christmas 1967 was to be a time of family reunion at Park House. Frances and Johnnie had agreed to set aside their differences for the sake of the children. Sarah and Jane would be home and their grandmother Ruth would be there as well. The youngsters looked forward to visiting their home, but once there, they found a tense atmosphere. Their parents barely spoke to each other except behind the closed doors of their father's study.

At the end of the holiday, Frances prepared to take the younger children back to London with her. With no prior warning, Johnnie refused to allow them to go. Shocked, Frances argued and pleaded with him, but finally conceded temporary defeat and left with a promise that she was going to sue for custody of all four children. Sarah tried to explain to Diana what "divorce" and "custody" meant, but at the age of 10 she hardly understood the terms herself.

After the older girls returned to West Heath, Johnnie placed Diana and Charlie in a school in King's Lynn. The governess they loved had been dismissed because of her loyalty to Frances, so when they were home they were cared for by a series of nannies. Their behaviour reflected their confusion and unhappiness as they put tacks on chairs for their nannies to sit on, locked maids in bathrooms and threw their clothes out the window. And Charlie's night-time crying resumed.

Diana was protective of her little brother, holding his hand tightly as they trotted over to the cemetery in Sandringham where their infant brother was buried and put flowers on his grave. Their father sometimes visited the nursery for tea, but their times together were strained.

In April 1968, Peter Shand Kydd's wife sued him for divorce on the grounds of adultery, naming Frances as co-respondent. The tabloids were filled with stories of the lovers' trysts.

Ruth was beside herself. Affairs weren't unusual in aristocratic circles, but discretion was the cardinal rule and her own daughter had broken it. When Frances and Johnnie had first discussed divorce, Ruth had been against it. However, now that it seemed unavoidable, she persuaded Johnnie to fight Frances for custody of the children. Although he was reluctant at first, she convinced him that he needed to prove he was the injured party in the breakdown of the marriage. It was the only way he could protect himself and his children from future social repercussions.

Ruth then persuaded the headmistress of the King's Lynn school to agree to testify that Frances never bothered to check on her children's progress and didn't reply to letters from the staff, which proved how uncaring she was. The fact that Frances had been making constant efforts to communicate with Johnnie to keep tabs on the youngsters was glossed over, along with her continuing pleas for him to allow Charlie and Diana to live with her.

Ruth was determined to make sure Frances's transgressions wouldn't harm her own relationship with the royal family, who at that time regarded divorce as taboo. Ruth had made big plans for her grandchildren and their future, and she refused to let her daughter destroy those plans before they could be set into motion.

Frances, having no idea what her mother was up to, went ahead with her custody petition. She assumed she would win because mothers usually did, unless they were proven to be abusive. Anyone who knew Frances as a parent could attest to the fact that she had never abused her children and was kind and loving towards them. She was confident enough in her ultimate victory to have reserved places for Diana and Charlie at their London school.

The day Ruth testified in court against her daughter, choosing her facts carefully to portray Frances as an unfit mother who had walked out on her husband and children for the sake of an adulterous affair, Frances knew she'd been defeated. No judge would believe that a woman would turn against her own daughter except for a very good reason.

Ruth firmly believed she did have a good reason. Frances's behaviour was not to be tolerated, and Johnnie had to be vindicated in the eyes of the royal family. When the judge awarded custody to Johnnie, Frances collapsed.

She must have longed for her father during those dark days. He wouldn't have allowed his daughter to be betrayed. He would have protected her and her children.

Her one remaining hope was her divorce petition, to be settled after the custody question. When the time came, Frances cited Johnnie for cruelty but he hit back with her adultery, already established in the Shand Kydd divorce. Johnnie won again. With his mother-in-law's help, he went on to make sure Frances was branded, in the eyes of society and the public at large, as a "bolter" who had walked out on her children without a backward glance.

Frances would manage to rebuild her life. Her children would come to love Peter Shand Kydd and look forward to holidays with him and their mother in Australia, and later in Scotland, where life was casual and carefree. But no one would emerge unscathed from the bitterness, least of all the Spencer children.

Goodbye, England's Rose

"Strange though it may seem, Diana's funeral was probably the proudest day of my life as a mother," Frances said after her youngest daughter had been returned to Althorp to be buried in the "Round Oval", a small wooded island in the middle of a lake on the estate. "Proud of her; my daughters, who were rock steady in their readings, and my son, who gave the ultimate tribute of brotherly love for her."

Frances and Diana had been out of touch for four

months. A misunderstanding caused by the constant pressure of a life played out in the public eye had created a rift, but no one close to the women believed their estrangement was permanent.

When Frances's phone had rung at two in the morning, she'd grabbed it quickly, assuming it was Diana – the only person who ever called at such an ungodly hour. Finally, she'd thought, finally they would be close again. But it hadn't been Diana on the line. The caller had brought news of an accident in a tunnel under the streets of Paris.

The healing of the rift would have to wait for another time and another place.

Epilogue

Some people have claimed that they've seen ghosts at Althorp.

It would be nice to think it's true. Imagine a gathering of female spirits, an ethereal hen party to welcome the newcomer, Frances, who passed over on 3 June 2004.

It could be held in the Picture Gallery amid all those portraits of Spencers and Spencer relatives, so the guests could walk along and admire one another in their earthly forms and the grand finery of their temporal beings.

Penelope could regale the others with her descriptions of great lords and ladies trying to eat with forks. Dorothy could show them the room she roofed over, once an open courtyard where Cavaliers clattered up on their massive chargers. The naughty ladies of the court of the Merry Monarch could spice up the evening with the juiciest gossip imaginable, and Fanny Work could regale them with stories of Americans in Paris.

The confusion of so many Lady Dianas and Georgianas would lead to some hilarity. Perhaps the Diana who became Princess of Wales would team up with her mother, Frances, to dance for the assembled spirits accompanied by Georgiana on her harp and Ruth at the piano – yes, even Lady Ruth Fermoy. This would be a place of forgiveness, of understanding that the human heart is fallible and has its reasons.

Cynthia, the grandmother Diana claimed as her spiritual guide in life, would smile and applaud in all the right places. Sarah Marlborough and Bess of Hardwick, however, would sit off by themselves, fondly shaking their heads at the antics of the youngsters while swapping tales of the great business deals they'd pulled off, beating the men at their own game.

The party would go on until dawn, then fade into the morning mist over the East Midlands, when the revellers would drift back to their husbands and lovers – or both.

Until next time.

Further Reading

Foreman, Amanda. *Georgiana, Duchess of Devonshire.* London: HarperCollins, 1998.

Hibbert, Christopher. *The Marlboroughs.* London: Viking, Penguin Group, 2001.

HRH Prince Michael of Albany. *The Forgotten Monarchy of Scotland.* Element Books, Ltd., USA Great Britain, Australia, 1998.

Pearson, John. *Blood Royal: The Story of the Spencers and the Royals.* London: HarperCollins, 1999.

Plowden, Alison. *Women All On Fire: The Women of the English Civil War.* Great Britain: Sutton Publishing Limited, 1998.

Riddington, Max and Gaven Naden. *Frances: The Remarkable Story of Princess Diana's Mother.* London: Michael O'Mara Books Limited, 2003.

Spencer, Charles. *The Spencer Family.* London: Viking, Penguin Group, 1999.

Waller, Maureen. *Ungrateful Daughters: The Stuart Princesses Who Stole Their Father's Crown.* Great Britain: Hodder and Stoughton, 2002.

Acknowledgements

This book is a small sampling of the tales I found when I looked into the family background of the late Princess of Wales. My fondest hope is that it might whet the reader's appetite for more. Of the sources listed in my bibliography, I'd like to note several that I found particularly interesting.

The current Earl Spencer, Diana's brother Charles, has written a lively history, *The Spencer Family*, in which he shares fascinating details from the unique perspective of a member of the dynasty. The earl also tells the story of his family estate in another book, *Althorp: The Story of an English House*.

Blood Royal, by John Pearson, focuses on the relationships between various Spencers and their monarchs, culminating in the merger of the two families when Diana married the Prince of Wales and gave birth to William and Harry, the first Spencer progeny to be in line for the throne.

Women All On Fire, by Alison Plowden, describes the experiences of the courageous heroines of the English Civil War.

Royal Survivor, by Stephen Coote, offers a fascinating view of the court of Charles II, and *Ungrateful Daughters* by Maureen Waller presents the events of the subsequent reign and deposing of James II from the viewpoint of the exiled Stuarts.

Christopher Hibbert's *The Marlboroughs,* Ophelia Field's *Sarah, Duchess of Marlborough,* and Amanda Foreman's *Georgiana, Duchess of Devonshire* bring some of Diana's most colourful ancestors to vivid life.

Bookshelves everywhere groan under the weight of volumes about the Princess of Wales. Two of the sources I most enjoyed were *Ever After* by Anne Edwards and *Frances, The Remarkable Story of Princess Diana's Mother* by Max Riddington and Gavan Naden.

My thanks to the Oakville Public Library for having so many wonderful history books to choose from.

And to my brilliant Altitude editor, Pat Kozak, I will be eternally grateful.

Photo Credits

Cover: Princess Diana courtesy of AP Photo / Denis Paquin; Georgiana Spencer, Duchess of Devonshire, courtesy of Mary Evans Picture Library

About the Author

Gail Douglas has written 14 contemporary romance novels published by Bantam/Doubleday/Dell of New York, but has always been drawn to historical biography – or rather, as she calls it, historical gossip. She loves discovering the quirks, ambitions, passions and fears of the people involved in important events of the past and watching their characters take shape as unique individuals living their personal dramas.

Gail started her professional career as a teacher and particularly enjoyed enlivening history classes with tales of Canadian adventurers. Altitude Publishing's *Amazing Stories* series includes her book, *Étienne Brûlé: The Mysterious Life and Times of an Early Canadian Legend*. Her husband, Tom Douglas, has also written three books in the series: *Canadian Spies*, *D-Day* and *Great Canadian War Heroes*, all with a World War II setting.

Gail and Tom live in Oakville, Ontario.

ISBN 1-55265-900-3